HAUNTED NEWAYGO COUNTY

MARIE HELENA CISNEROS

Haunted America

Published by Haunted America
A Division of The History Press
Charleston, SC
www.historypress.com

Front cover: Former I.J. Robinson Block. *Author photo.*
Back cover: Kimbark Inn, circa 1920s. Once held a speakeasy said to have been frequented by Al Capone. *Published by the Eagle Postcard Company, New York, New York. Public domain.*

First published 2024

Manufactured in the United States

ISBN 9781467157018

Library of Congress Control Number: 2024936753

CONTENTS

ACKNOWLEDGEMENTS

First of all, I would like to extend a wholehearted thank-you to Eric and Krystal Johnson of Flying Bear Books & Creperie for their kind hospitality and for hosting a book research/ghost story forum. Through their willingness to support this project by inviting the community to attend, they opened up many new avenues of exploration. I was able to learn much about the area's history as well as learn more about some of the local ghost stories and legends. It was very enjoyable and useful, and I felt very welcomed by all. My thanks to Eric for also sharing his story.

My sincere appreciation goes out to Jan Smith, Nadine Andrews and Sandi Bernard for their useful information and stories about the Indigo Inn & Down Under Bar. I also want to thank Jan for sharing her story.

In the interest of protecting privacy, I am not able to properly credit all sources; nevertheless, I am sincerely grateful to everyone who attended and shared their knowledge and stories, both named and unnamed, as well as to those who were kind enough to give me impromptu house tours.

I am very grateful to the knowledgeable and friendly staff at the Grant Area District Library for taking the time to assist me in finding information for the Grant hospital chapter. While time did not permit me to peruse any library books, I could not help but take note of how bright and cheery the library was. One often thinks of libraries as stuffy and dull; this one is nothing of the sort.

I would also like to thank the entire staff and the volunteers at the Heritage Museum of Newaygo County for their kindness and help. Museums are amazing places, filled with culture, art and artifacts from bygone eras. As such, they have much to teach us—if we are willing to learn. In addition to the immensely enjoyable time I spent at the museum looking at the wonderfully executed and informative displays, everyone was very friendly and knowledgeable. This hidden gem of a museum is on par with museums many times its size and well worth a visit for anyone interested in learning about Newaygo County and Michigan history.

Conducting research might seem a tedious endeavor, and occasionally, it is. Nonetheless, the time I spent in Newaygo while gathering historical information and taking photographs was very pleasant, made all the more so by the benevolence that was extended to me. Thank you one and all; you are all appreciated.

INTRODUCTION

If you are someone who likes to visit places that are wholesome and give you the warm fuzzies but also enjoy exploring places that are a little bit mysterious, then Newaygo County may be the perfect place. For if the stories can be believed, Newaygo County has a few ghosts in residence. Nestled between the sprawling Manistee National Forest and the blue expanse of Lake Michigan is Newaygo County. Miles of lush, green woods, farmland and sparkling shallow lakes dot its surface. Although much of its past has been lost to the annals of time, its rich historical past played an integral part in Michigan's history nonetheless. Many of the towns and villages have historic sites dedicated to the county's beginnings; sixteen places, sites or buildings have been designated as historic sites. There are also numerous celebrations and events throughout the year, several of these specifically for commemorating historical events. Newaygo County was first populated, early in its prehistory, by the Algonquin tribes of Native Americans, predominantly the Ottawa. The county's European pioneering history dates to the fur trade and the lumber industry, with some of the first settlements in Michigan. Its beginnings are impressive enough that they would make any historian sit up and take notice. However, beneath the characteristic historical facts filled with industry and enterprising people, Newaygo County also has a history of the paranormal kind, one that is filled with accounts of ghosts, hauntings and legends.

There are five cities, twenty-four townships, five unincorporated communities and one village in the county, each of them with a unique past and character. What might come as a surprise to some of the folks living in the thirty-five towns and communities within its borders is that a number of them are believed to be the source of ghostly tales, haunted buildings or other mysterious lore from days long gone. While time has moved on and these towns and cities have grown from the days when oxen-pulled wagons rumbled down dusty, unpaved roads and lumberjacks felled majestic pines, the tales of hauntings, spirits and the mysterious remain. In fact, over the years, numerous mysterious legends and stories have circulated throughout the county. A number of them are probably familiar to many county dwellers, such as the story the ghosts at Dudgeon Swamp in White Cloud, Michigan, where victims of the Dudgeon family were murdered, or the tales of mysterious sightings and paranormal encounters in the Manistee National Forest. The former La Belle de la Riviere bed-and-breakfast has long been rumored to have had a few ghostly visitors. Then there's the apparition of a little boy said to precariously make his way across the top of the dam in Croton, Michigan. In the city of Newaygo, which at one point burned almost completely to the ground, strange tales of ghostly encounters are told, from stories about an eerie sense of foreboding at the decayed ruins of the Big Red Mill to the tale of a wrathful, screaming spirit said to haunt a long-abandoned house on a hill. These are the types of extraordinary stories that give paranormal researchers and ghost hunters a tantalizing taste of the mysterious side of Newaygo County. Understandably, they may be the tip of the iceberg, as many stories remain untold. Consequently, only time will tell how many more mysteries may be found hidden in the forgotten lore of Newaygo County.

Newaygo County is the quintessential essence of the American experience. The history of Newaygo County, which predominately developed and grew as the lumbering era took hold in Michigan, speaks volumes about the colorful tapestry that is our country's foundation. As the county was settled at various times throughout its long history by Native Americans, explorers, fur trappers, lumbermen and pioneering settlers, it is distinctive in its makeup of explorers and pioneers, who came from all parts of the country and the world. Some of the first came from Europe, Scotland, England and France. In the ensuing years, the area became vitally important, as the vast number of logs that came out of its forests helped the growth of settlements around the country and abroad. Every year, whole forests' worth of logs were cut from the woodlands of Newaygo and sent down the Muskegon River to be cut into lumber, creating wealth as well as work for thousands. While this created jobs, built settlements and made wealth for many, it also had a

Logging brands display. *Heritage Museum of Newaygo County. Author photo.*

devastating effect on the area's forests, many of which never recovered. In the winter of 1840, the first logs were sent coursing down the Muskegon River from the Mill Iron by the Merrill Mill in Newaygo. That same winter, John A. Brooks sent logs that were cut above the Mill Iron down to "the flats," then downriver to Muskegon Lake. In April 1864 alone, 160 million logs were harvested. By 1883, with much of the county's forests dwindling and only the northern regions retaining any extensive areas of pine, the county revitalized itself by turning its attention to agriculture, hydroelectric power and marl mining. But throughout the changing times and uncertainty, the pioneering spirit of Newaygo County prevailed, and it continued to reinvent itself.

> *Newaygo County is justly proud of her pioneer record, and, so far as possible, the compilers of the biographical sketches have striven to honor the representatives of that period as well as those of to-day. Labor and struggle, performed in the light of hope and the earnestness of honest endeavor, established the county on a permanent basis, and is rounding up a period of glorious completeness. Her villages are creditable and her agricultural community is composed of the best grades of humanity.**

---

* *Portrait and Biographical Album.*

9

If nothing else was said, this quote would give you a pretty good idea what Newaygo County is like: a land of hardworking, strong, enterprising pioneering people who, with their down-to-earth sensibilities, are willing to eke out a living and persevere no matter what the odds.

There are numerous lakes and streams in Newaygo County, but one of its crowning jewels is the Muskegon River. It was well known by the French early on and had been charted on maps even before the 1700s. The Muskegon River, Michigan's longest and most diverse river, arises from Houghton Lake in Roscommon County. It flows in a southwesterly direction 216 miles through ten counties, emptying into Muskegon Lake. This majestic river has been known by various names throughout history, such as the "Riu a la Biche" (by the French). It was known as the Maticon, the Masticon and the Mastigon (by Native Americans). Along its shores is abundant wildlife, including white-tailed deer, waterfowl, eagles and otters. For the Native Americans, the river was their lifeblood, sustaining them throughout the changing seasons. These early inhabitants often made their camps by water. With the abundance of fish and wild game in the surrounding forests to sustain them, the Muskegon River was perfect. This was also an ideal place for the fur trappers who came later. For some years after the county was settled by pioneers and lumbermen, many of the Native Americans groups remained, and contact with the settlers was generally good. Trade relations between the two groups remained amiable for the most part. While lumbering, urbanization and land development took its toll on this majestic river, efforts have begun to restore this priceless natural resource back to her natural beauty.

Newaygo County is nicknamed the Heart of Western Michigan. Created in 1836, it spans 862 miles, 48 of which are covered by the 230 natural lakes within its borders. The river watershed drains an area of land over 2,300 square miles and covers ten counties. It is bordered by Lake County to the north, Mecosta County to the east and Oceana County to the west. Muskegon County lies southwest of it, Montcalm to the east-southeast and Kent County to the southeast. Cities, communities and towns in Newaygo County include Newaygo, White Cloud, Brohman, Fremont, Grant and Bitely. Croton, Denver, Grant, Bridgton, Ashland, Sherman and Beaver are a few of the townships within the county.

Exactly how Newaygo was named is a bit murky. Some say it was named for Nah-way-gon, the Chippewa chief who signed the Saginaw Treaty of 1819 and was renowned for his bravery. Other stories say that it stems from a time before European trappers had even set foot in the county and is derived

Native American loom display. *Heritage Museum of Newaygo County. Author photo.*

from the Algonquian word for "much water." "Much water" seems to be an apt description for the county, as water was indeed significant to its settlement. Being situated near the Muskegon River, which was an important travel route for people as well as goods, Newaygo was looked on by explorers and settlers as prime land. Moreover, with its wealth of forestland and easy access to the river, Newaygo soon became a vitally important asset to the burgeoning lumbering industry. Almost immediately, sawmills were built near the river in order to transport the lumber. Being able to quickly transport logs downstream was vital to the industry until railroads were built in the ensuing years. By 1837, the county had its first sawmill, and

City of Newaygo street sign. *Author photo.*

soon, logs cut there were floating down the Muskegon River to be shipped to Chicago out of Muskegon. A second mill was built at Croton. For many years, from the late 1800s onward, lumbering determined the pattern of settlement of the county, with mills cropping up along the riverbank—that is, until the area's forests were exhausted. These first mills were dependent on power supplied by the river as well as other, larger streams. The lumber was cut close to the mills or near streams, making it easier for the logs to be floated down to the mills.

Thus, the Muskegon River was a key method of travel and a means to transport supplies and equipment as well as lumber. By 1875, the loggers had been sawing away at Michigan's forests for over forty years. Waterways were the principal way of transporting lumber until the first logging railroad was built in Clare County. The difficulty in hauling logs was the underlying motivation for railroads finding their way into the county as well as the rest of the state. Up until that time, logs were dragged on the ground and then put on sleighs or wagons in order to get them to the sawmills. This method was not only time-consuming, tedious and unreliable; it was also expensive. Logging companies quickly found it more dependable to transport lumber by railway. Moreover, since transportation was no longer dependent on river levels, logging became a year-round industry. While there were several early railroads operating in Michigan, one of the most well-known in the area was

The Courtright Hotel, Newaygo, Michigan. Destroyed in the fire of 1883. *Photochrome postcard, circa 1900–08. Published by Curt Teich & Co. Chicago, Illinois. Public domain.*

the Lake George and Muskegon River Railroad, owned by Winfield Scott Gerrish, which began operating in 1877. Gerrish promoted his railroad widely, which helped generate further development of logging railroads in Michigan as well as the rest of the country. Oftentimes, these railroads followed paths that had earlier been traveled by Native Americans. In fact, many of the county's early roads had also followed Native American trails. Early on, trappers, lumbermen and settlers had used the Old Indian Trail to transport logs and supplies. This trail was later called the Newaygo to Northport Road on surveys, becoming part of the stage line. Eventually, it was renamed State Road. As the settlements became more populated, more roads were made connecting towns and cities. One of the earliest roads was from the Merrill Mill area to Muskegon, cut by John Chidister. Chidister went on to build a bridge across the Muskegon River. The settlement that sprang up in that area became the town of Bridgeton.

The dawning of Newaygo County's settlement began in 1836, when Hiram Pierson and Henry Pennoyer headed up a small group of land speculators from Chicago who planned to occupy the entranceways of all streams north of the Grand River going to Manistee using "squatter's rights," until such time as they could make claim to it when it came on the market. This group was formed to operate in land and timber. Taking possession of the proposed claims as quickly as they could, Pennoyer and others built cabins along Muskegon Lake. Similarly, others set up homesteads farther north. In 1837, the area was still sparsely inhabited, and Mitchell Charleau, a French trader, was said to be the only non–Native American living at that location. Clark Knight and Augustus Pennoyer soon found a location with access to water power that was ideal for building a sawmill. Charleau, who operated a trading post above the Muskegon Fork, was hired to take the men up the Muskegon River. Charleau was hired because the river was blocked with floodwood, creating hazardous conditions, and someone was needed who knew how to navigate the river as well as help avert any other dangers. Charleau was a seasoned fur trapper, and his knowledge of the river as well as the territory was vital. During the course of their trip, the small group decided to make a stop at what is now the city of Newaygo. It was here, at the mouth of a creek, that Augustus Pennoyer and Jack McBride put down claims, which they named Pennoyer. Not long after, McBride built a cabin and established a claim, becoming the first settler in the county. Later, he sold his claim to George Walton. McBride subsequently staked a claim on land near what later became Brooks Creek. Pennoyer then partnered with Alexander Fulton of Muskegon, forming the Muskegon Lumber Company. Ultimately, this lumber company laid the groundwork for the first permanent settlement in the county. By the 1890s, the lumber industry had essentially disappeared, along with most of the woodlands. After the county's abundant forests were depleted, the area's fertile soil was next eyed as a means of revenue and growth, with the idea that agriculture would yield even greater wealth than the lumber industry had. By the late 1800s, Newaygo County had over one thousand farms, and thirty thousand acres of land were growing a vast variety of grains, fruits and vegetables.

Following McBride's lead, it wasn't long before others with the pioneering spirit and the desire to set down roots came to Newaygo County. After Michigan became a state and the Homestead Act was passed in 1862, land became available to anyone willing to homestead a property for five years. Consequently, many people took advantage of this opportunity to become landowners. Unlike the fur traders and trappers, who picked up and went where the best furs could be found, the settlers came to stay. Although the blossoming settlement was not without its profiteers and opportunists who would occasionally venture in looking for a means to profit, for the most part, the homesteaders wished to establish a permanent home base. This pristine land with its abundant, unspoiled forests and wildlife, brimming with beaver, deer and other fur-bearing animals, had rapidly drawn the French trappers, or *coureurs des bois* and then subsequently the lumbermen.

The Muskegon River, Riverfront Park, Newaygo, Michigan. *Author photo.*

City of Newaygo commemorative monument, Brooks Park, Newaygo, Michigan. *Author photo.*

They were all champing at the bit to make a profit from Newaygo's bounty but weren't, for the most part, the sort to stick it out for the long haul. It wasn't long after passage of the Homestead Act that pioneer wagons loaded down with supplies, family possessions and dreams were headed to the county, which was still very much uninhabited. Starting in 1837, the settlers came, many in wagons pulled by oxen, loaded down with their possessions: anything from pots, pans and spinning wheels to plants, seeds, chickens and a milk cow tied to the back. The journey would not have been an easy one, by any means. Wagons were slow and cumbersome, often breaking down and having to be abandoned. The settlers also had to be wary of swollen rivers, illness, inclement weather and flooded roads that were mere paths at best. Tradesmen came, bringing the knowledge of their craft as well as the tools of the trade. In addition, there were farming folk and others with varying abilities and skills willing to stake out a claim and work the land. Soon, many others came, building shops and businesses, many of which still exist. One of the first to homestead in Newaygo County was John Manning, who staked his claim in Denver Township in 1868. Another intrepid early pioneer was George Rosenberg, a former buyer for Ryerson Hills Lumber in Muskegon, Michigan. George Rosenberg operated one of the oldest family-run businesses in White Cloud. Rosenberg had settled in White Cloud after buying the hardware store there, which he eventually expanded into a full-service lumberyard. Interestingly, George also sold automobiles, which were actually assembled on-site. He sold his first car to one Wes Hepinstall. It seems Rosenberg operated the ultimate in a full-service business for the times, as he also taught Wes to drive the car he purchased. That is service above and beyond what one sees today.

Some came to work in the sawmills or at cutting lumber. It takes an indomitable spirit to uproot kith and kin to strike out into the unknown, but this is what the settlers of Newaygo County did, in spite of the dangers of a sometimes inhospitable wilderness. Like the pioneers who forged their way out West, Newaygo County's pioneers sought new opportunities, new ventures and a place to call their own. While we cannot be sure what prompted many of them to come here, what we can be sure of is that these first settlers had fortitude and courage. They were determined and here for the long haul come hell or high water, which often came in these parts in the form of floods.

Despite the hardships those first settlers endured, they found the area idyllic. Even now, the county has much to offer, with its wide-open spaces and nature, laid-back atmosphere and small towns full of friendly people.

Oxen yoke and plow display. *Heritage Museum of Newaygo County. Author photo.*

If you've ever lived in a small town, you know they have a lot going for them. Who wouldn't want to live somewhere without the hectic rush to beat five o'clock traffic every day? For most of the communities in Newaygo County, spending precious time sitting in bumper-to-bumper traffic is not really a problem, and for the most part, everything is a stone's throw away. A common misconception about living in a small town is that there is nothing to do. However, there are plenty of things to do in the towns of Newaygo County: comforting, joyful things like holiday fairs and community events, high school sports games, backyard get-togethers or just sitting on your front porch shooting the breeze with neighbors. Furthermore, there is nothing better for the soul than being in nature, and Newaygo County has nature in abundance. Countless people near and far find ways of enjoying its riches, like camping, hiking, fishing or going on color tours. Clearly, these are all wonderful advantages of living in smaller communities, and they continue to attract people. However, the one quality that sets Newaygo County apart from most urban areas, which tend to be less cohesive in nature, is an underlying ideal of "community." For Newaygo County folks, it is not just an abstract idea; it is a way of life. It is the underlying glue that holds the county and its people together. For example, if someone is going through a rough patch for any reason, it doesn't take long for someone to step up to lend a helping hand. Whatever the reason, people look out for each other. This could be in the form of starting a fundraiser, giving a lift, bringing sick person meals or just lending a listening ear.

Truly, living in Newaygo County in those early years must have been quite charming. This is evidenced in part by the creation of an annual county fair early on. During the late 1800s, going to the county fair was a pleasant outing for folks in the county. The fair was the creation of the Newaygo County Agricultural, Horticultural and Mechanical Society. Some of the board members were Sullivan Armstrong, David W. Squier, William Edmunds and Frances H. Hooker. The fair was held in the back of George King's store on State Street. It drew people from miles around to purchase handmade crafts and baked goods, enjoy races or look over livestock and farm products. One year, fairgoers were treated to a baseball game between the Newaygo, Casnovia and Sparta ball clubs, with the Newaygo club winning. Another time, a hot-air balloon was planned, but the weather didn't cooperate. Unfortunately, due to financial problems and a dispute over location, the annual fair was terminated, and the society disbanded. Clearly, there are not too many things that make us more nostalgic and bring out a greater longing for simpler times and country living than a county fair. Unfortunately, in many places, county fairs, with all their charm and delight, have gone the way of the horse and buggy or the analog phone, never to return. Luckily, though, through the efforts of the Newaygo County Agricultural Fair Association, this is not the case in Newaygo County, and this cherished part of Americana is alive and well in the "north country."

Thus, for those longing to leave the big city lights behind for a simpler way of life, living in one of Newaygo County's cities or towns might truly be idyllic. Being polite and saying hello to your neighbor when you meet on the street is still commonplace. Unfortunately, this sense of community seems to be noticeably absent in big cities, for the most part. That frenetic hustle and bustle of urban life is hard to find in Newaygo County, and that suits people here just fine. Furthermore, people here also support their local businesses. Many of the local shops and businesses are family owned and go back many generations. Undoubtedly, Newaygo County is a land of hardworking, reliable people, many living ordinary but good lives, going about their day-to-day business of working, playing and spending time with friends or family. Furthermore, they are also people who have been through hardship and many changes. They don't scare easily and probably don't spend a lot of time worrying or thinking about ghosts, haunted places or the paranormal. Nevertheless, the murky tale of the Dudgeon Swamp murders might give them a chill if they found themselves alone at night in the vast regions of the Manistee Forest. Perhaps they might wonder what they would do if they ever came across the spectral apparition of the mysterious girl in black while walking on a trail or caught a glimpse of the ghostly figure of a little fisher boy atop the Croton Dam. They may have heard the legend of Screaming Ethel, who is said to haunt Whiskey Wood House, or felt a sense of gloom and foreboding while venturing onto the grounds of the Old Red Mill, long abandoned and decaying. Admittedly, these strange goings-on probably wouldn't scare them—unless they believe in ghosts.

Chapter 1

Days of Decadence: Ghosts of La Belle de la Riviere (Riblet House)

The light from a crystal chandelier cast a warm glow over the bejeweled and elegant revelers dancing feverishly below. Ladies in fringed dresses swayed to-and-fro as they jitterbugged to the music, while the men's shoes clicked to the rhythm on the floor. Others sat with glasses of bootleg whiskey in hand or partaking of the lavish buffet. Very serious-looking men, dressed to the nines in expensive tailor-made suits, fedoras and shoes with pearl-buttoned spats, stood in small, intimate groups around the room. They talked deals in hushed tones as they smoked cigars, the smoke rising up in a cloud above their heads.

Suddenly, the scene vanishes into a mist. The laughter, music and distant footsteps echo softly through the house, and then they quickly fade away. This swanky roaring-twenties party with its gangsters and flappers dancing and enjoying themselves at Riblet House, later known as La Belle de la Riviere, in all likelihood never happened. Nevertheless, there is some evidence that many years before it was a popular bed-and-breakfast in the town of Newaygo, this elegant mansion was associated with Al Capone, one of the most notorious gangsters in history, and that he often came to the area. There are also rumors that it is, or was, haunted, with people claiming to hear strange murmurs and music in some of the rooms as well as spectral footsteps echoing in the basement.

La Belle de la Riviere, or the Beauty of the River, was one of the names of a popular, elegant bed-and-breakfast in the heart of the town of Newaygo currently known as the Newaygo bed-and-breakfast. The mansion has been

La Belle de la Riviere bed-and-breakfast, Newaygo, Michigan, as seen from the garden. *Author photo.*

an integral part of Newaygo's history since early on. Newaygo, situated in western Michigan, was the first settled community in Newaygo County. Like the county, the town of Newaygo is said to have been named for the Chippewa chief Nah-way-gon, or its name may derive from the Algonquian word for "much water." It covers an area of almost four miles and is one of the most populated towns in the county, with about 2,400 people living there. While the area was well-known to Native Americans who lived and thrived near the Muskegon River as well as the French trappers who traded with them as early as the 1700s, Newaygo became a formal settlement in 1836 when the Pennoyer brothers and others staked out a claim. Augustus Pennoyer, Frederick Pennoyer and Alexander Fulton of Muskegon chose to build a sawmill at the mouth of the creek they named Pennoyer, thus creating the first permanent settlement in the county and beginning the area's lumber industry. Having the river so near enabled Newaygo to thrive as an epicenter for lumbering throughout the county as well as the state. At one time, there was a fourteen-foot dam built across the Muskegon River, a wagon bridge and a dam across Pennoyer Creek. The power generated by the creek water that rushes downstream in powerful cascades was found useful in the lumber and other industries. Presently, there are three dams on the Muskegon River: Rogers, Hardy and Croton. John Brooks staked a claim in the area soon after the Pennoyer brothers and is said to have been the first settler in Newaygo. During the booming lumber era, Newaygo flourished as a major hub for logging due to its proximity to the river. After the forests had given all they could, agriculture, marl mining and cement production sustained the area's economy for a number of years. Although much of the commerce and manufacturing has gone into decline since those boom-town days, Newaygo has found new ways to revitalize its economy, including successfully reinventing itself as a popular tourism and recreation site in recent years.

The town of Newaygo, a sparkling Michigan jewel, is almost hidden from sight, and one's first glimpse of it often surprises. Traveling along M-37

City of Newaygo. *Author photo.*

toward town, the road first dips into a valley, curves around and then climbs a hill whereupon the smiling city greets you warmly. Rounding the corner onto State Street, one finds picturesque and charming historic buildings that stand as a testament to the town's glory days. On the Newaygo County Exploring! website, Newaygo artist and longtime resident Gabe Schillman calls it a "truly magical place," writing:

> *The historic district of this town still features all of the old world charm and design; restored vintage buildings, bustling mom & pop storefronts, a century old train bridge that spans the river—still in regular use, riverfront parks and walking paths, and a quaint museum that tells the whole story in detail. Here, there are happy people—some local, some passing through, enjoying river floats, nighttime walks, shopping, or eating at one of the many downtown establishments.* *

Places like River Stop Café, Sportsmans Bar, Downtown Threadz and others flourish in buildings that are rich with history and stories. This delightful town, carved out of the wilderness so long ago, possesses an enchantment that few cities have ever been able to achieve. Indeed, Newaygo continues to have much to offer, with abundant opportunities for picture-perfect memories to be made. Here, you can experience spring bursting with flora and fauna, summers filled with fun along the river, the vibrant gold of autumn leaves and whimsical pumpkin patches and a heartwarming Christmas celebration where State Street is aglow with lights and cheer is had with friends and neighbors. This is a place where the cares of big-city life fall away and the commitment and warmth of community thrive. The Muskegon River, which, remarkably, meanders through the northern part of the town, draws tourists and the sports-minded like a magnet from near and far. Numerous inns and cabins have cropped up along its shores to accommodate those wishing to enjoy all the enchantments that nature has to offer, whether it's camping, fishing, hunting, hiking or just enjoying the landscape. With its slow, twisting course, the river is ideal for kayaking, rafting, or canoeing, and campers can stay at the various parks and campgrounds located at or near the river. A state game area covers over 8,400 acres of land in Newaygo and Muskegon Counties, giving licensed hunters access to white-tailed deer and waterfowl hunting. The river has also grown increasingly popular as a prime fishing spot, with plentiful stocks of planted Chinook salmon, migratory steelhead

---

* Schillman, "A Truly Magical Place."

River Stop Café decorated for Christmas Walk, Newaygo's annual holiday event, 2021. *Author photo.*

and trout. The White River and the headwaters of the Pere Marquette are also favored fishing spots. In fact, the county is known for some of the best fishing in the country, with fisherman flocking to its lakes and streams, where they can try their luck at catching their fill of pan fish, trout, steelhead or salmon. Boating on the river has been a favorite pursuit right from the start. Surprisingly, there was even steamboat travel on the Muskegon River from 1869 until 1873. The first steamboat was *Lizzie May*, which, regrettably, sank about a year after service began. The second, the *North Star*, made regular weekly runs from Muskegon to Newaygo, and another steamer, the *Newaygo*, also made regular trips between the cities. Both ships were put to use as freighters and, by 1871, had more freight than they could transport.

Winding through Newaygo, the Muskegon River carves a crescent-shaped path through the landscape. High bluffs on either side of the river create a valley below. Within this valley lies the city of Newaygo, rising above the level of the river on a natural terrace. At one time, a railroad passed between the river and the town, close to the river's edge, passing through the valley down a ravine. With streets both ascending and descending the natural hills, meadows and grass-covered bluffs on either side of the river, the town of Newaygo creates a remarkable vision, even as it did in its infancy as a blossoming village. On State Street, a number of the present buildings were built in 1883. After a fire destroyed much of the town, all buildings in the business district were required to be made of brick, thus ensuring their survival.

Incorporated as a village on March 16, 1867, Newaygo first came into being as a settlement when a group of land speculators from New York built the dam across the river and constructed a large mill on property they had previously bought. Soon after, the Newaygo Company—Amasa B. Watson, A.F. and H.J. Orion, A.N. Cheney and L.L. Anns—brought equipment and tools from Grand Rapids. A large number of men to work in the mills was also needed. This had the effect of quickly growing the population, and the Exchange Hotel was soon built. Brooks House was constructed a few years later. The mill started by the Pennoyer brothers was later run by Robert W. Morris and Samuel Rose. Being the first official settler, John A. Brooks is considered the father of Newaygo. He and Sarell Wood platted the village in 1853. Brooks had come to Michigan from Stanstead, Canada, where he worked at one time as a hotelkeeper. Brooks was said to be a dynamic and enterprising individual and was held in high regard in his business dealings, choosing to do much of the day-to-day work himself. He was also prominent in politics and was elected to Newaygo County's first board of supervisors in 1863. With the market for lumber increasing at a phenomenal pace in Michigan and elsewhere, the manufacture of lumber became immensely profitable. Thus, Newaygo became ground zero for the logging industry in the North. Seeing an opportunity for further growth, Brooks secured improvements on the Muskegon River flats near Muskegon in order to float rafts. This was so successful that steamboats were then able to traverse the river, making trips to Newaygo during the warm months. As population and travel needs increased, funds were also appropriated to construct state roads.

Soon, a road was made to Traverse City and the road to Grand Rapids was improved. In all, 187 miles of roads were built to and from Newaygo, with E.L. Gray constructing almost 100 of them. In addition, with the lumber industry flourishing, Newaygo trade also began to blossom, resulting in the need for the construction of two hotels. These were soon crowded with guests. The roads between Newaygo and Muskegon and Newaygo and Grand Rapids were soon overflowing with lumbering equipment, tools and other commodities, readily supplied by Newaygo merchants. A stagecoach line was begun and made daily runs to Grand Rapids, with a trip every other day to Muskegon. This route was later extended to Big Rapids. Indeed, Newaygo was soon bustling with industry.

Over the ensuing years, Newaygo experienced both boom and bust. In 1857, the Pennoyer Newaygo Company had to reorganize as a business. With the Grand Rapids and Indiana Railroad's construction of a rail line going to Cedar Springs, a large share of the travel was diverted there.

John Brooks memorial, Brooks Park, Newaygo, Michigan. As the first settler in the county, Brooks is considered the "Father of Newaygo." *Author photo.*

Consequently, it became clear that the village's continued success hinged on connecting with the Grand Rapids railway system. With the help of many of Newaygo's prominent citizens, including W.D. Fuller, D.P. Clay, E.L. Gray and S.K. Riblet, a railway line from Grand Rapids to Newaygo was finished in 1872, thus securing the town's prosperity. This line, a branch of the Chicago & Michigan Lakeshore system, was extended to Big Rapids, with its final destination Traverse City. After the railroad was finished, attention was turned to improving State Street, which was where the majority of shops, offices and public facilities were located. When the county's forests' bountiful supply of pine was exhausted and the lumber industry fizzled out, industrious eyes turned to the area's ample agricultural resources as a source of revenue. This effort was greatly enhanced by the use of water power supplied by the rivers and creeks to run machinery. As time went on, the rapidly flowing streams of the Muskegon River and the Brooks and Pennoyer Creeks became a boon to manufacturing, as they had in the lumber industry in years past.

Once again, the wheels of industry and commerce slowed, and manufacturing receded in importance, to the detriment of the area's economy and citizens. Even so, the pioneering streak is still very much present. Even now, the town is reinventing itself as a popular tourist destination and is once again blossoming in a new direction. This popularity is well-deserved. Newaygo is a friendly town with a heart of gold, opening its arms to those who flock to the area as a place of outdoor adventures, scenic views, relaxation and tranquility. Of course, with the arrival of tourists, sports enthusiasts and vacationers comes the need for accommodations. One popular place for those seeking accommodations is the Newaygo bed-and-breakfast. A vital part of Newaygo's rich past, this stylish and unique Victorian-era home is favored for its nearness to area restaurants as well as prime fishing spots; it's also close to area shops, restaurants, bars, a conference center and a museum. Nearby is access to the Muskegon River and outdoor activities, including tubing, rafting, boating and fishing. Those willing to drive a little ways can participate in amusing seasonal activities like fruit picking, mushroom hunting, snowmobiling or cross-country skiing, as well as horseback riding, hiking or biking the many trails.

This elegant mansion, previously known as the Riblet House, was called the La Belle de la Riviere when it first became a bed-and-breakfast in 2006. It was built in 1868 by Solomon Kuiper Riblet, an early pioneer of Newaygo. Riblet was born in 1901 and died in 1996, aged ninety-four. Solomon Riblet came to Newaygo in 1856. After working in the building trade for about three years, he was employed by Leonard & Woolley, druggists, after which he became a manager of S.W. Matevey, a mercantile that sold groceries, clothing, hats, caps, dry goods and other essentials. Three years later, he bought the store. Solomon married Jennie Putnam Day from Morean, New York. The couple had five children: Grace, Fred, Ruth, Mattie and Lavinia. Riblet was very much involved in the development and success of Newaygo (which was then still a village), serving in many capacities, including being street commissioner and part of the group that funded and commissioned building the railroad. He was also a member of the local Masonic lodge. He was known to be sympathetic and kind, being very active in charity work. He was looked on by his peers as a man with unimpeachable integrity and high principles with keen business acumen. Riblet was believed to be the first in the area to own a sailboat and greatly enjoyed taking his family sailing. His social and business relations with his peers and others in the community made him a most valuable asset to Newaygo.

Nestled in the heart of downtown Newaygo, La Belle de la Riviere is a testament to Newaygo's resiliency and vitality, as it was one of the few wooden buildings that survived the fire that devastated the town of Newaygo in 1873; thus, it is one of the oldest houses in the county. In addition to the seven large guest rooms, this impressive Victorian house has an expansive living room, a dining room, a billiard room and a piano room, as well as space for outdoor gatherings. The Italianate style arose in popularity during the Victorian era, dating to the 1840s and peaking around 1888. After sweeping across Britain and Europe, Italianate architecture quickly became popular in the United States also. One of the chief catalysts for its popularity was the introduction of style pattern books that streamlined architectural designs and manufacturing, bringing down prices. Many of these charming and elegant structures can still be found in neighborhoods in parts of Ohio, New York, California, Louisiana and Washington, D.C. It is believed that the first known structure built in the Italianate style was designed in Shropshire, England, by John Nash, who was inspired by the romantic and naturalistic designs of the Italian countryside. The Italianate style was very much sought after for its fresh take on classic Greek architecture, which was felt to be overly formal and pretentious. The Italianate style of architecture was greatly influenced by the Renaissance and the gardens and villas of Italy, as well as by Victorian-era Romanticism, which skillfully unified the homespun essence of a Tuscany farmhouse with the symmetry of an Italian villa. Other architects and landscapers, enraptured by the grandeur

La Belle de la Riviere bed-and-breakfast (former Riblet House), Newaygo, front veranda. *Author photo.*

of the Florentine and Italian Renaissance followed suit. Before long, they, too, began using similar motifs to bring the quintessential charm of Italian palazzos and Tuscany country homes into their designs.

The use of the Italianate style had the advantage of giving designers a variety of layout options and, with the advent of the Industrial Age, many of the iconic elaborate accents could be easily mass-produced. Another advantage is that Italianate houses were priced to accommodate both people of modest income as well as wealthier patrons and could be changed to fit a variety of structure types, ranging from rowhouses or city brownstones to large, elaborate houses. Vibrant gardens, picturesque grottos and sprawling landscapes were an integral part of the Italianate concept, connecting the home to its surroundings and nature. If done well, this gave one the sense of being part of a living Renaissance painting. Italianate-style homes and buildings are usually two to four stories tall; their roofs are slightly sloped with overhanging eaves, decorative brackets and wide cornices. Windows are tall and arched, and interiors are spacious. Entrances have details such as brackets and columns, some with one-story porches that usually have detailed woodwork. Landscaping on the grounds has whimsical elements, such as follies and grottos. Porches, fences and balconies are liberally decorated with manufactured cast-iron or metal elements. I have had the pleasure of touring the mansion several times, as well as learning some of its history. It is stunningly beautiful. The mansion and its history are exceptionally remarkable, and it is now listed as a Historic American Home.

If the only thing that one remembered about the history of La Belle de la Riviere was that it remained standing after fire destroyed the town, it would be worth one's while to know. However, that is only a small part of it. The property has a lesser-known history, one that played an important part in several aspects of Newaygo history. For starters, it is believed that the house was once owned by Al Capone's lawyer, who had family in the area, and that Capone was a frequent visitor. With his lawyer owning property in Newaygo, it stands to reason that Capone might have good reason to go there from time to time. Evidence for this is somewhat murky, but given Newaygo's central location between two of the biggest cities in the state, it would have been the perfect midpoint for Capone's bootlegging enterprise. Indeed, stories and rumors have circulated for years that Capone was a frequent visitor to Newaygo and its environs. It is widely known that Capone left his mark in cities and towns around Michigan, predominately in the Detroit area, and it is believed that Capone or his gang did away with over one hundred people in the Newaygo area. This suggestion fits in with long-held rumors that Mystery Lake is the site of many of his victims' remains. The area is said to have been favored by Capone not only because of its prime location for bootlegging but also because one of Capone's favorite brothel workers lived very nearby. However, in all likelihood, Newaygo would have interested him greatly, too, for it held a little-known secret, one that few outside the area knew. It is believed that, at one time, there were tunnels beneath the Riblet House used as part of an Underground Railway system for slaves or ex-slaves seeking safe passage to freedom. If anything would have drawn a bootlegger to Newaygo, it would have been these tunnels. Believed to also have run under Newaygo's streets and sidewalks to other buildings and beyond, they would have made the job of hiding and transporting illegal alcohol relatively easy. Local history and stories indicate that the notorious bootlegger Capone and his gang did make use of the tunnels to transport alcohol during Prohibition. They were also said to be the site for private parties and events. Nothing says "party spot" like a hidden tunnel with access to a bar. Knowing that the 1920s was a time of decadence and excess, one would have to assume that there was indeed some socializing going on, even if it had to be done on the sly. Additionally, one local establishment said to have been frequented by Capone and his cohorts was a bar called the Snake Pit. The Snake Pit was in the basement of the River Valley Inn, a hotel built in the 1880s. It burned to the ground in 1991.

Al Capone, also known as Scarface, was an American gangster who controlled organized crime during the Prohibition years, running everything from bootlegging to prostitution in Chicago. His syndicate, called the Chicago

Al Capone's May 16, 1929 mugshot. *Pennsylvania Department of Corrections/FBI. Wikimedia Commons. Public domain.*

Outfit, ran unchecked from 1925 to 1931. Capone is considered by many to be the most notorious gangster in United States history. He was born and raised in Brooklyn, New York. Capone took to a life of crime at an early age. After dropping out of school at fourteen, he worked odd jobs, including bowling alley pin boy, candy store clerk and ammunition plant laborer. Regrettably for society, toeing the mark at a conventional job and working his way up was not for him. While working those odd jobs, he was also a member of the Forty Thieves Juniors and the South Brooklyn Rippers, two juvenile gangs that committed petty crimes and vandalism. He then joined the James Street Boys, which was controlled by Johnny Torrio. Johnny would become Capone's mentor and a lifelong associate. Capone got the nickname Scarface when a man named Frank Galluccio slashed his face for making a crude comment about Galluccio's sister. Capone soon made his name in Chicago and elsewhere by controlling the bootlegging, prostitution and gambling rackets, sometimes referred to as the Chicago Outfit. His was a name that could strike fear in those who opposed him—and for good reason. Capone had no compunction in maintaining that control by taking out rival gangs or others by ruthlessly gunning down anyone who stood in his way. His methods, while cold-blooded and heartless, proved fruitful, and at one time, he was estimated to be worth $100 million. Nevertheless, Capone's empire was not to last. The Chicago Outfit dynasty crumbled when he was indicted on twenty-two counts of tax evasion and conspiracy to violate Prohibition laws. In 1923, he was found guilty on three counts, fined $50,000

La Belle de la Riviere bed-and-breakfast (former Riblet House), Newaygo, at the top of the stairs where music was heard. *Author photo*.

and sentenced to eleven years in prison. He began serving his sentence in the Atlanta federal penitentiary but later was sent to Alcatraz. Capone's reckless personal lifestyle also caught up to him, and he was released to a Baltimore hospital for treatment of paresis brought on by late-stage syphilis.

Gone were parties, luxuries, cohorts, money and power. At the end, body and mind ravaged by the paresis, he had the mentality of a twelve-year-old. He died at his Florida home in 1947, a virtual recluse.

Because of haunting rumors and reports of inexplicable sounds of jazz or 1920s music being played in some areas of the house, as well as strange thuds and other mysterious noises, the Riblet House is said to have been investigated by a paranormal group for a popular syndicated television show. After their findings, priests were consulted, who performed an exorcism. Since that time, all paranormal activity is believed to have ceased. One curious aspect of the music was that it seemed to be heard best under certain atmospheric conditions. Atmospheric conditions have been noted in other paranormal cases to be a factor. Another factor was that the music seemed to triangulate, yet the precise location could not be accurately pinpointed. This all added to the inexplicable nature of the phenomena.

What are we to make of the stories of ghostly voices in the guest rooms, ethereal music when no musician is playing and odd noises heard in the basement in the middle of the night? Arguably—if we were to assign a paranormal cause to it—perhaps it was the spirit energy of a long-ago piano player that was heard, imprinted in the environment. S.K. Riblet had a piano room, so it's quite possible that someone in his family played the

La Belle de la Riviere bed-and-breakfast (former Riblet House), looking down from the second floor. *Author photo.*

piano. One could also imagine it stemmed from a jazz musician playing jaunty tunes at a twenties party, his tunes so rousing that they remained. Music can be powerful; possibly, its vibrational energy imprinted itself on the environment, especially when the pianist was feeling the emotion of the music. Were people really hearing the murmuring of a ghostly conversation in the guest rooms? Some might suggest they were spectral guests who had "checked out" but never left. What of the strange noises said to emanate from the basement? Perhaps the tunnels held spiritual energy left over from the countless hours the men spent in them transporting bootleg alcohol. Was this place haunted at one time? There are some who believe that it was. Others believe that the ghostly voices, strange music and inexplicable thuds had logical explanations, although one would have to think that if paranormal investigators believed there was something unusual going on, then perhaps it was so. Fortunately, the strange goings-on have ended thanks to the intervention of the priests, and La Belle de la Riviere is no longer considered to be haunted. Whether or not you believe it was ever haunted, there is no question that this popular B&B is a beautiful, welcoming place to come and enjoy yourself. There is no doubt that it hosts some wonderful events. Nevertheless, it would be grand if we could step back in time, even for a few moments, to experience the past. Even if it is just a mirage, it is fascinating to imagine that, at one time, gangsters and their molls danced the night away at the lawyer's house, and Al Capone was right there, drinking bootleg whiskey and having the time of his life. It would have been one great party to crash, if it weren't for all those tommy guns.

CHAPTER 2

GOOD NIGHT, LADIES:
GHOSTS OF THE INDIGO INN &
DOWN UNDER BAR & GRILLE
(OLD KIMBARK INN)

Bereft of hope, alone, maybe even a bit angry, the shadowy, frail beauty silently wandered down the hall, her long, sweeping dress trailing behind her. As a bordello worker at the Kimbark Inn, she was presumably passing the time before her next client. Conceivably, she was also searching for a way out of her precarious situation. Little did she realize that her days of working in the hotel had ended long ago, as the Kimbark Inn no longer exists. In fact, neither does she. She is but a spirit, destined to walk its halls for eternity. She, of course, is not even aware that the halls she roams are those of the Indigo Inn. For a number of years, the Indigo Inn (formerly the Kimbark Inn, Rathskellers and, before that, the DeHaas Hotel), was rumored to be haunted by an assortment of spirits, from ghostly apparitions of women believed to have been brothel workers to a rather menacing male spirit to a small child who wanders the hallway. Unfortunately, the Indigo Inn has also gone the way of its predecessors and has been closed for a number of years.

In its heyday, the Indigo Inn was a delightful bed-and-breakfast in the heart of Fremont, having been restored to its prior glory days reminiscent of the Kimbark Inn. After undergoing years of stagnation throughout the seventies, it was in poor condition. Through determination and a flair for design, the owner restored it to its former charm, as well as adding some other innovative touches. For starters, the Kimbark's turn-of-the-century allure and old-world charm was brought back by lovingly and painstakingly reproducing its English pub décor and fixtures. Some features of a typical pub—if one could ever be called typical—are rustic, antique furnishings, décor and architecture in warm, woodsy colors from the twenties, Victorian or medieval eras. Pubs ooze comfort and cordiality. They are charming and quaint, and the menus often feature traditional comfort foods that incorporate a locale's heritage and customs. While not strictly adhering to the British model of a pub, the Indigo Inn had the soul of one, with a sense of community and warmth at its heart. Perhaps this is why the spirits continue to stay at the inn. In addition to renovating the Indigo Inn, the Down Under Bar & Grille, located in the basement, was made over to create an eclectic, safari-themed atmosphere. The Indigo Inn closed in 2012 but, at one time, held a coffee bar, tearoom, spa, gift shop, art gallery, lower-level bar and a pool. The art gallery, while small by some standards, was a unique and engaging place where artists and crafters could display their works. There was also a billiard room downstairs separate from the bar.

If you could ask townspeople about the strange goings-on at the inn over the years, they would probably tell you that the Indigo Inn was indeed haunted. The Indigo Inn Bed and Breakfast was located on Division Street, in the heart of Fremont, the biggest city in Newaygo County. It was formerly the Rathskeller as well as the Kimbark Inn, although it originally

DeHaas Hotel, circa 1900–1910. Once a very popular hotel. *University of Michigan Bentley Historical Library. University of Michigan Library Digital Collections. Public domain.*

began in the late 1800s as the DeHaas Hotel. Built by John DeHaas, it was one of Fremont's most popular places to stay. Tragedy struck, and the hotel burned down in 1887. Undeterred, DeHaas rebuilt, this time in the style of a British tavern. At that time, the DeHaas included a saloon, billiard room and dining room, as well as a barbershop. Among its guests were many politicians and businessmen. It is believed that a bordello occupied the third floor of the inn starting in the 1900s and continued into the 1930s. It was at this level that a lot of spiritual energy was said to be felt, some of it rather negative. A number of people died in the fire that destroyed the first hotel, among them the women who worked in the brothel. The hotel changed hands a number of times over the years. In 1923, it was purchased by the Fremont State Bank. A year later, the bank, along with investors, built the Kimbark Inn. The Kimbark Inn, like its predecessor, the DeHaas, rose to prominence—or notoriety, depending on your moral stance. Apparently, this popularity was because it went above and beyond in its willingness to cater to its guests, including supplying them with the company of "ladies of the evening." Arguably, much of the Kimbark's popularity occurred during a time when pleasure-seeking was taking root throughout the country, giving rise to the speakeasy.

While the twenties and thirties have gone down in history as an era of hedonism and decadence, it was also the peak of Prohibition and the Great Depression. In 1920, the Volstead Act was ratified, closing all bars, saloons and taverns in the country. After this, it was illegal to sell intoxicating drinks containing more than 0.05 percent alcohol. However, people are inventive; those who wanted to imbibe found a way. That was part of the enticement: alcohol was forbidden fruit, and in spite of the government prohibiting its manufacture and distribution, it was not illegal to have it for personal use. Thus, the liquor trade made its way underground and so did "bootleg" alcohol. The speakeasy was born. It is not really known who coined the term *speakeasy*, but it swiftly became a household word. Possibly it evolved from the secretive manner in which patrons gained entry into these clandestine establishments. One would only be admitted by giving a secret word or name to the lookout guarding the door through a small window cut in the door. Undoubtedly, having a speakeasy in the building had some bearing on the Kimbark's popularity. Moreover, the Kimbark's speakeasy was another Newaygo County establishment that ended up being associated with Al Capone.

Capone quickly took advantage of Prohibition. As law enforcement had ineffective support from the government due to lack of funding, organized

KIMBARK INN, FREMONT, MICHIGAN

Kimbark Inn, circa 1920, Fremont, Michigan. Once held a speakeasy said to have been frequented by Al Capone. *Published by the Eagle Postcard Company, New York, New York. Public domain.*

crime started controlling many aspects of making and distributing alcohol with a major connection to speakeasies. This control was ruthlessly enforced by criminals, racketeers and bootleggers using violence and other illegal abuses, with the worst being Al Capone. It was believed at one time that Capone employed a thousand gunmen as well as having a good portion of Chicago's police force in his pocket. Over the ensuing years, the illegal manufacture and smuggling of alcohol throughout the United States continued pretty much unabated despite efforts to subdue it. In addition, Prohibition encouraged the proliferation of other crimes, and a considerable amount of money was made through those avenues. Capone's bootlegging, racketeering, prostitution and speakeasy syndicate earned him millions. Like many other establishments around Michigan and the country, the Kimbark served illicit alcohol provided by the bootleggers, and as he was for these other establishments, Al Capone is believed to have been a supplier. In fact, Capone reputedly made frequent stops at the Kimbark. The bar was in the basement and was accessed by using the steps leading down to the lower level. This out-of-the way entrance was found useful during its Prohibition days. After Prohibition was repealed, the lure of the speakeasy waned, and by the 1950s, the Kimbark had lost its glamour as a popular drinking spot. The Kimbark was sold in the 1950s and again in the 1970s, after which the inn fell into disrepair. During this downward spiral, it became a frequent hangout for drug dealers and drifters.

Throughout the years, many strange things were reported by staff and patrons at the Indigo Inn and Down & Under Lounge and Grille. Some have claimed that the whole building is haunted, and at one time, ghost tours were conducted at the inn. Staff who had worked upstairs felt quite sure that it was haunted. Some of the inexplicable events were thoroughly investigated by paranormal researchers and authors Kathleen Tedsen and Beverlee Rydel, along with author Amberrose Hammond and the late Tom Maat, two of Michigan's best paranormal investigators. Investigators reportedly believed that the building was experiencing more than one level of residual spiritual activity and that not all of it was positive. For example, one area in a darkened storage room near the kitchen was believed to give off some intensely negative energy, although energy noted in the downstairs lounge was felt to be of a positive nature. Investigators were also able to pick up positive EVP results. Tedsen and Rydel thoroughly chronicled these paranormal episodes, as well as the investigation's results, in *Haunted Travels of Michigan*.

In June 2023, an informal forum-type event was held at Flying Bear Books & Creperie, hosted by bookstore owners Eric and Krystal Johnson, as part of a *Haunted Muskegon* book signing. People were invited to share their favorite local ghost stories as well as relate their own paranormal experiences. A few people familiar with the Indigo Inn attended. They were able to share some of their experiences with the inn and related having experienced or witnessed strange activity while working there. One story involved a plumber who came in to do some work on the third floor. He wasn't there long before he packed up his gear in a hurry and left as quickly as he could; his face was ashen, and he was obviously terrified of something. Another harrowing incident happened one night when Sandi Bernard, a musician, was getting ready to perform. She had placed her guitar securely on its stand on the stage. Suddenly, the guitar flew off the stand and violently struck the floor, as if picked up by unseen hands. A number of people witnessed this firsthand, including Nadine Andrews. Understandably, they were all stunned. Nadine said she had seen shadowy figures of a man, both upstairs as well as the basement. Not all this energy was good. Sandi felt that the entity upstairs was quite malevolent and seemed to be particularly so toward women.

There appears to have been much paranormal activity at the inn and bar, including people seeing apparitions and hearing discarnate voices and objects being misplaced or inexplicably moved. The spirit forms of a woman, a little girl and two men have been described. Many of these shadowy forms and apparitions were witnessed by both staff and patrons of the inn and lounge. The spirit of a young girl would be seen standing by a screen door or heard giggling and slamming the door shut. Her spirit was also felt or seen in the hallway on the second floor. Some of the other spirits mentioned included a very tall, thin man with dark hair and a beard; a tall, thin man wearing a hat; and the shadowy figure of a woman who looked forlornly out of an upstairs window. Certain areas of the second floor were reportedly host to a lot of spiritual energy. Some of the energy seemed rather negative, with people seeing an intimidating, dark, shadowy form and feeling that it wanted them to leave. The lower level was also reported to have had a lot of spiritual manifestations, with apparitions appearing in the hallway only to inexplicably disappear into a storage room. This room was also sensed to be the source of some negative energy. Some of these spirit forms were felt to be female, perhaps the residual energy forms of the bordello workers. A lot of energy could be felt on the landing but also in some of the rooms. On the upper level, in rooms that were closed due to renovations, this energy became rather foreboding and heavy. In addition, one investigator saw an apparition or shadow form in the hallway. Staff sometimes felt the hallway was a bit creepy, and there were a few parts of the inn that seemed to actually give off some negative energy. One of the male spirits may have been someone who died in the fire that destroyed the hotel. A few of the spirits believed to haunt the building are Romney, Old Bob, Elizabeth and Sem, as well as many unknown brothel workers and patrons.

Although the indecent goings-on at the DeHaas Hotel and the Kimbark back in the day might make one tend to think that Fremont was quite a racy place, that is not the case. On the contrary, it was and continues to be a town of hardworking people with good values. Given the volatile forces and circumstances that brought on the Great Depression, with its poverty and an unsure future bearing down on society, one may be able to see how people would have liked some respite, even for a short time, from its effects. Furthermore, the seediness that Prohibition invited in was not to last. Soon the wheels of time righted themselves, and the devil-may-care attitude and wanton hedonism of the roaring twenties ended with no more than a whimper. Soon, Fremont, like the rest of the country, regained a sense of balance and structure. Consequently, while Fremont was not immune to grasping ahold of the allure of the speakeasy and its pleasures, its solid roots built on community, pioneering spirit and enterprise took hold again, enabling it to prosper and thrive.

No. 2. Main St., Fremont, Mich.

Top: City of Fremont in the 1960s. *Postcard. Published by AVERY Color Studios, Saranac, Michigan. Used with permission.*

Bottom: City of Fremont in the 1900s. *Postcard. Published by Will P. Canaan, Grand Rapids, for L.E. Norton. Fremont, Michigan. Public domain.*

Fremont's ability to thrive in spite of its growing pains has been with it since the beginning. Like many other towns in Newaygo County, the first people to settle the area were Native Americans. Starting out as a village, it is now the largest city in Newaygo County. It spans almost five square miles, with over four thousand people living there. A little over three miles of this is landmass, and one and a half square miles is covered by water; Fremont Lake is the second-largest lake in the county. In 1855, Fremont was organized as a township, which then separated into Dayton and Sheridan Townships in 1867. The first group of pioneers to set down roots here was led by Daniel Weaver in 1855. He and Wilks S. Stewart ventured here from Hesperia with the dream of owning property. The way was not easy, as much of the area was still wilderness, and previous efforts to obtain land had been unsuccessful. After meeting John Brooks of Newaygo, Weaver was able to obtain a solid lead on buying land. After being shown a tract of available land by Hiram Butler, who owned a Newaygo hotel, Weaver made his way up to Newaygo County. Greatly satisfied with the spot, Weaver and his group purchased almost one thousand acres of land, and Fremont was born, first as Weaverville in 1854 and then as Fremont Center. After buying the property, Daniel came back with a small group who helped him build his home and clear the land. Later, Dutch immigrants from Muskegon and Holland followed suit. The Weaver house later became the township's first post office and school, and Weaver eventually became the township's first supervisor. Fremont was named to honor John C. Frémont, who was an explorer, an officer in the military and the first ever Republican candidate for U.S. president.

Fremont was another Newaygo County village that soon became part of the growing lumber industry. Its growth, like that of Newaygo, Croton and White Cloud, was spurred on by the lumber industry. Conversely, its eventual demise had a detrimental effect on the local economy as well as the population. After its decline in the 1860s due to overharvesting of the forests, the Civil War and a forest fire, Fremont's lumber mills took a major hit. Fortunately, Fremont was able to revitalize itself through courage and diligent enterprise. Soon, many businesses and companies began cropping up to take up where lumbering left off, with one of the most successful businesses being the Gerber Products Company. Gerber was founded by Frank Daniel Gerber in 1905 as the Fremont Canning Company, to can produce from local farmers. The company soon became very successful, with sales exceeding $1 million in 1917. It expanded its facility to year-round production in 1915. In 1928, it began making baby food, using the "Gerber Baby" logo. Twelve years later, when baby food sales exceeded adult canned goods, the company stopped producing adult canned goods. Its name was changed to Gerber Products Company in 1941. Additionally, the Gerber Foundation, created later on, has been instrumental in improving the infants' and children's quality of life for many years. The mission of the foundation's research projects includes seeking solutions to health and nutritional problems that affect children, as well as prevention and treatment of diseases. Over the years, Gerber Products Company—and its iconic label—has become a household name throughout the United States and abroad, making Fremont the "Baby Food Capital of the World." Fremont holds an annual National Baby Food Festival, with over fifty thousand people attending each year.

While the festival is undoubtedly a huge draw, there are plenty of enjoyable things to see and do in Fremont. As in many other areas around Newaygo County, there are abundant resources for recreation, with miles of trails for hiking, parks for picnicking and access to boating, swimming or fishing. Arboretum Park is a serene place with a wandering path, featuring native Michigan greenery including trees, shrubs and wildflowers, which students of nature find helpful, as well as those seeking the quiet solitude of nature. Other Fremont parks also have much to offer. For those looking for arts and entertainment in Fremont, the Dogwood Center for the Performing Arts is an excellent choice, with a black box theater that can comfortably accommodate 420 patrons. Anyone with an interest in astronomy might enjoy a trip to the Stephen F. Wessling Observatory near Fremont. Of course, a great restaurant is always a good draw, and two of Fremont's popular dining establishments should be on anyone's bucket plan. Newaygo County residents vote the Blind Squirrel Tavern's burgers the best in west Michigan. Another one of the specialties on the menu is nachos topped with the tavern's "famous Squirrelffallo sauce." The menu doesn't state whether any actual squirrels are involved in said nachos—either making them or being part of them. Undoubtedly, this is just a catchy name. Given that they are nachos, they sound appetizing, nonetheless. The Brew Works, with a variety of delectable food, unique craft brews and drinks, as well as access to a nine-hole golf course, is another local favorite.

From pioneering lumber town to a thriving, warm small town with a suburban feel, the Fremont community continues to blossom, with the help of kind people whose pioneering spirits are evident in its hospitality and caring environment. This is a cozy, serene town full of friendly folks: a small town with a big heart. Perhaps it was that pioneering spirit that prompted someone to take a run-down hotel and built it into a bustling, friendly place to go for an evening out or an overnight stay. It is said that the spirits were treated with gentleness and compassion at the Indigo Inn. Even though they were the ghostly shadows of the departed, they were as well received as the living guests. Sadly, no one is there to turn down the bedsheets in the guest rooms or make cookies for the guests any longer. The owner has passed on, and the Indigo Inn's doors have been shuttered forever. Guestroom lamps no longer cast their glow for weary guests. Still, the eerie nightly vigils go on throughout the inn's halls and rooms. These ethereal shadows or residual energies, whatever their source, continue to make their rounds. Shadowy men in top hats stride the halls, and the beautiful, ghostly ladies of the evening still wander aimlessly. Good night, ladies.

CHAPTER 3

GUARDIAN SPIRITS OF THE WOODS: GHOSTS OF THE MANISTEE FOREST

It was midnight, the bewitching hour. The full moon, high in the sky, cast a silver glow over the hiker, weary from a long day's journey through the heart of the forest. He trudged on, searching for a good spot to make camp. After finding a suitable clearing, he quickly put up his tent and settled in. As he sat there in his tent, he noticed that an uncanny stillness had enveloped the forest. Earlier, he had heard the usual sounds of wildlife, like the scurrying of a foraging rabbit making its way through the underbrush, the occasional hoot of an owl and the rhythmic croaking of tree frogs. Now, the woods were eerily silent. Cautiously, he opened the flap of the tent and looked around. Squinting through the darkness, he saw a huge, shadowy, doglike figure dart behind a tree. He told himself it was his imagination but quickly shut the flap and zipped it up as far as it would go, just in case. Next, in the distance, he heard a low, unearthly howling and then a strange whistling. This uncanny howl struck terror in his heart. He had heard the strange stories of werewolves and dogmen stalking their prey but never believed any of them. At home in the city, his logical mind would have told him these things do not exist, but alone at night, in the dark recesses of the forest, it was easy for him to believe such things to be real. With heart pounding and eyes filled with terror, he sat and waited, trying not to think about what was lurking in the dark… watching. Several days later, when he hadn't shown up to meet his friends, a search party was sent out. When they arrived at his campsite, there was no sign of the hiker.

If you have ever been camping, you know that sitting around a campfire sharing stories—maybe a story such as this—is an enjoyable way to spend an evening. The glow of the fire lights up the campers' faces, and a sense of awe and wonder soon envelopes them. Usually, these stories involve something strange or frightening happening to campers such as themselves. One would think that their vulnerability would make them less apt to partake of such stories, but this is not the case. Many people often enjoy being scared—as long as they know it is not real.

The problem, though, is that some people believe stories like these are true. In fact, they believe that forests, including the Manistee National Forest, are home to spirits, elementals or other unknown beings who can either help or harm humans if care is not taken. Since time immemorial, there has been the belief that the forest is home to a multitude of spirits or strange entities that appear from time to time. It is even believed that forests themselves can be haunted. If so, could someone or something be haunting the Manistee National Forest?

Practitioners of earth-based religions are familiar with elementals, believing them to be the spirits of the four elements that make up our material earthly world: fire, earth, air and water. One such elemental is a woodland spirit, said to be a protector of the trees and animals. This spirit entity goes by many names. In Slavic countries, where it is said to principally watch over wolves, it is known as the Leshy. Other stories have it being a servant of the bear. Descriptions of the Leshy are varied. Some stories describe it as being half human and half animal, with a green beard or covered in moss, with claws and horns. Like other mythological forest spirits, the Leshy are said to be tricksters or shapeshifters. They cast no shadow and are said to be able to change form or size, appearing as a human or a forest animal. They can become as large as a tree or as small as a blade of grass at will. Even more bizarre is that they appear very large when seen from a distance but small up close, a supernormal feat that defies logic. It is said that the arrival of the Leshy are accompanied by wind as they make their way through the forest. They can mimic the sound of a human voice or the sound of rustling leaves or branches. They can sometimes also be heard laughing, singing or whistling. While one might find it exciting to have an encounter with a Leshy, crossing one can have disastrous results, from falling ill to being carried off, never to be heard from again.

Manistee National Forest (MNF) lies between Lake Michigan and Lake Huron, covering a total area of 540,187 acres, part of which is in Newaygo County. This vast stretch of forest spans the counties of Newaygo, Lake,

Manistee, Wexford, Mason, Muskegon, Mecosta, Montcalm and Oceana. There are numerous trails, parks and campgrounds within its boundaries, principally along designated areas such as the Pine, Manistee, Au Sable and Pere Marquette Rivers. One exceptionally unique site in the forest is Briar Hill, although there are no marked trails leading to the top. Visitors wishing to climb to its summit have to make their own trail through the brush. The hill has the distinction of being the highest elevation in the Lower Peninsula, reaching 1,706 feet and affording a clear view of the surrounding region. The hill also boasts a multitude of wildlife, including black bears, coyotes, deer, fox, porcupines, beavers and river otters. Covered with partially grown hardwood, it is believed to date back to the Ice Age. The hill was created when melting glaciers left deposits of sand in its wake. Owing to its proximity to Lake Michigan's volatile weather patterns, the hill tends to be subjected to lake-effect snowfalls during the winter months. With its abundance of wildlife, wide-open spaces, family-friendly parks and campgrounds and glorious scenic views, it's no wonder Manistee National Forest is a popular destination for hunting, fishing, camping, boating and hiking, as well as cross-country skiing and snowmobiling. Its numerous trails include the North Scenic Country Trail, which joins with the Manistee River Trail. This trail makes a twenty-three-mile loop, connecting the North Country Scenic Trail to the Manistee River Trail. This trail usually takes several days to complete, oftentimes requiring hikers to set up their campsites at night.

The combined Huron-Manistee forests are managed by a team of specialists, including biologists, archaeologists, botanists and fire and timber experts. The team is responsible for managing the health and harvesting of endangered or sensitive species' habitats, as well as prescribed burns. Although administratively it is joined with the Huron National Forest, the two are separate units, and the Manistee itself is separated by towns and private property in many areas. The MNF was established by President Franklin D. Roosevelt in 1938 by acquiring tax-forfeited lands after the end of the logging boom, with the goal of replanting cutover areas. After being cleared of all salable lumber, some areas were covered with stumps and fallen tops, making it unsuitable for farmland. Unfortunately, forest areas that had been burned over had not yet regenerated even by the 1930s. During the 1920s, the movement toward preservation of wildlife, conservation and reforestation began to gain steam in Michigan. In 1933, President Roosevelt created the Civilian Conservation Corps (CCC). This program supplied labor jobs to unemployed young men during the Great Depression to assist with the development and conservation of natural resources within government-held rural lands. Workers from the CCC were employed to replant much of Michigan's decimated forests. The forest now contains a mixture of hardwood and pine trees, with red pine being the most abundant. The CCC planted rows of this species. Many of these trees stand seventy-five feet tall today and continue to be harvested for timber. The Kellogg Experimental Forest, with the largest adjoining expanse of red pines in North America, is within Manistee Forest.

Today, we sometimes think of forests as only places to spend a few vacation days camping, hiking or taking nature walks. However, in days past, while exciting to enter, they were also viewed with awe and entered with caution. They beguiled and beckoned but were rife with unknown perils and danger. It was understood that the forest could be friend or foe. The forest was mysterious, holding a sort of magic, although whether its magical spell would enthrall or harm depended on the reverence paid to it. Like everything in life, the forest held the good as well as the bad, both light and shadows. Also, forest creatures were often volatile in nature, and it was quite easy to get turned around. Thus, one could easily become a meal for a hungry bear or a wolf or get hopelessly lost. Adding to that were perils unseen and spiritual. There were mythical creatures, among them elementals or nature spirits tasked with protecting the forest and her creatures, said to always be on the lookout for anyone seeking to do harm or otherwise desecrate the forest. They were unpredictable and very protective of their home. No doubt things could turn out badly for those unlucky enough to run afoul of them. Like the villages of yesterday, cities, towns and villages of today are places where people seek refuge and stability, building homes and communities, and strive to live in relative peace and comfort. Villages and towns offered boundaries, stability and togetherness; forests offered the mysterious, the untamed and solitude. Being among others within a community offered a sense of protection and safety. For the most part, villagers were most concerned with putting food on the table and keeping the wolves from the door, both the financial kind and the fur-bearing kind. Yet another concern in more superstitious times was their belief that the forest harbored a myriad of mythical and wondrous beasts. Occasionally, a bold villager or two, bored with life in the village, would fearlessly—or foolishly—go in search of forest adventures. As often as not, some were never to be seen again. Then, as is the case with a few of the hapless folks who have tragically gone missing in our national parks, their fate was often unknown. The forest engenders abundance and all the fullness that nature has to offer, as well as all that is mysterious, wild and uncontainable. In truth, its dangers are real.

Of course, these dangers are as comprehensible to us now as they were to our ancestors. However, the idea that fearsome, monstrous or mysterious things lurk in the forest is now, for the most part, neither comprehensible nor believed. Belief in entities like skinwalkers, Dogmen, werewolves, fairies, spirits, gnomes, Leshy, and Bigfoot are scoffed at in our modern society. As such, we relegate them to campfire stories or tabloids. Nevertheless, encounters with spirits, strange beasts or entities or experiences of paranormal events that defy explanation have and do occur within the forest and elsewhere. For hundreds or thousands of years, forests have played a significant role in myths and legends, Manistee National Forest included. Undeniably, the Manistee Forest is one of Michigan's crowning jewels, but like other forests around the globe, it has been the setting of many legends and stories about supernatural creatures or spirits that wander the forest at night. In fact, some have claimed it to be a hot spot for things that go bump in the night—or things that howl, screech and crash in the night. Folk tales within the villages of yore that people grew up were filled with stories of ghosts, monsters and fairy folk who inhabited the forests. Tales told by the Ottawa, lumberjacks and trappers who lived and worked in the forest bear that out. The belief that magic can be found deep within the forest is also very common in folk tales around the world. That these mythical spirits or creatures also possess superhuman power is a common theme. While some of these mythical beings are helpful to man, others are not.

The forest has its own set of rules—rules that, if broken, could be fatal. It also has communities living and thriving within its depths. Since time immemorial, forests have been believed to be home to myriad mythological and mysterious creatures or spirits. In the past, many of these creatures were said to have been banished from society and forced to live as outcasts among the trees. Having been deemed violent or dangerous by villagers, they took refuge within the deep recesses of the forest, where they now reside. During the daylight hours, the canopy of trees, the lush underbrush and the lack of human habitation offers them protection. But when darkness falls, the mysterious creatures of the night come out of hiding to roam. These creatures are believed to come in the form of Bigfoot, Dogman and the even more ominous and evil wendigo.

Most people have heard of Bigfoot, although many do not believe he exists. However, Bigfoot has been seen in almost every single state within the United States. In fact, the idea that a large, fur-covered beast exists in the forests or mountains is a worldwide one. These creatures are called by different names—Yeti, Sasquatch, Yowi and, of course, Bigfoot—but have very similar properties. Over the years, researchers and cryptozoologists have gathered footprints, hair samples and scat that they claim is from Bigfoot, being quite convinced it is a physical being. While it may be comforting to think that Bigfeet, if they exist, are to be found in faraway forests, some people believe that this hairy, eight-foot-tall humanoid creature also dwells in the forests of Northern Michigan. Sightings of them have been reported for years, and numerous people claim to have seen fleeting glimpses of a Bigfoot or heard one crashing through the woods at night. Others say they have heard its ear-piercing call, likening it to the scream of the banshee. While Bigfoot is believed to keep well out of sight in the deep recesses of the forest, encounters and tracks have been reported within a mile of White Cloud and other towns. There have been over one hundred reports of alleged encounters with these huge, fur-covered bipeds, and many encounters are said to have occurred in and around the Manistee and Huron Forests. Remarkably, a Bigfoot was believed to have been captured on a trail cam near Beulah, Michigan, several years ago.

If one takes the eyewitness accounts and purported physical evidence at face value, they might make a good case for Bigfoot's being a physical reality. Of course, some people find the idea that there are huge bipedal creatures living in the Manistee Forest, or any forest for that matter, incredible and completely absurd. Yet even more incredible is the assertion by a few paranormal investigators that Bigfoot is not a living creature at all. He is, in fact, something akin to a ghost or interdimensional being. This idea differs from the premise that Bigfoot is a physical being. Bigfoot as ghost or interdimensional being stretches the limits of believability even among the ranks of paranormal researchers. Nevertheless, there might be something to that theory. Bigfoot legends have been part of Native American culture for thousands of years, giving credibility to the idea of his existence. Culturally, these Native American legends incorporate the spiritual with the physical world. Thus, the Native Americans interwove the Sasquatch's physical reality with the spiritual, believing that it had supernatural powers and could shapeshift or become invisible. Consequently, if we take Native American mythology into consideration, assigning Bigfoot a purely physical manifestation may be a bit tricky. Other mythologies may also support the possibility that Bigfoot is a ghost or interdimensional being, as Bigfoot would likely fit into the category of elemental or woodland spirit. Elementals, as the name implies, are believed to be an essential part of the material world and to have been in existence since the beginning. According to the legends and mythology of various cultures, within the ranks of the elementals are gnomes, elves, fairies and lake creatures. Sasquatch, skinwalkers and Dogman might also be part of the pantheon, although lesser known in their present characterization as elementals. Elementals are believed to be guardians of the natural world. There have been accounts of hunters or campers being harassed or attacked by some unknown entity while in the woods. If those accounts are true, then it is reasonable to imagine that these attacks were an effort by an elemental or guardian spirit to protect the forest.

While it is true that forestland usually covers an immense area, the "Bigfoot-as-Ghost" researchers find it a bit odd that although hundreds, perhaps thousands, of people go out into the woods to camp, hunt or hike every year, yet Bigfoot sightings are still very rare. Some of these researchers feel that the lack of sightings is more proof that Bigfoot is a ghost or spiritual entity. Additionally, they reason that because no one has ever gotten a decent photo or video of him, he does not exist as a physical being. On the other hand, there have been multiple photos and videos allegedly showing Bigfoot, although most have been found to be misidentification or outright hoax. In addition, no bones, fossils or bodies found have ever been documented as genuine. Again, that belief that Bigfoot is some form of spirit or interdimensional entity is not accepted by all Bigfoot researchers, who do in fact feel that some physical evidence, photos and videos obtained are genuine.

Flesh and blood or ghost, Bigfoot isn't the only scary creature said to lurk in the shadows of the northern Michigan woodlands. If the stories are to be believed, then one could also encounter a manlike creature with the head of a dog, aptly named Dogman. Michigan Dogman sightings have been reported since 1887. One incident reportedly happened in 1938, when a man claimed that he was attacked by wild dogs, one of which walked upright like a human; in another case, a Dogman was allegedly seen by two lumberjacks. And there's the wendigo, an evil spirit or supernatural creature also said to live in forests and near lakes. Stories and legends of the wendigo have come down to us from the folklore of the plains and Great Lakes Natives as well as some First Nations groups. The wendigo is based in and around the East Coast forests of Canada and the Great Plains and Great Lakes Regions among speakers of the Algonquian family of languages. The Native American tribes of the Great Lakes and Michigan forests, predominately Algonquin, Ojibwe, Odawa and Potawatomi, believed that all living things, including animals, plants, rocks, trees, etc., possess a spirit. Thus, they respected the spirits of each one, even the grains of corn, believing them to be gifts from the creator spirit, gichi-manidoo. This belief in animism was central to their way of life, and it not only governed humans, animals, plants and rocks but also inhabited sicknesses. These illness spirits could manifest in different shapes and forms, bringing either good or bad fortune or illness. The man-eating wendigo was said to have once been a human who had committed wicked acts in the past. The wendigo was greatly feared by the tribespeople, so much so that they even avoided speaking of it. Woodland tribes would paint their faces with war paint to protect themselves from it. The wendigo is often depicted as a malevolent spirit, sometimes as a creature with humanlike characteristics that possesses humans and invokes feelings of insatiable greed or hunger, a desire to eat human flesh and the propensity to commit murder in anyone who falls under its influence.

If being a malevolent, cannibalistic spirit wasn't bad enough, wendigos are also believed to have great supernatural power. The descriptions vary but have some common themes. The wendigo has been described as extremely tall with white, matted fur and a large head with large yellow fangs and a blue tongue. Both its hands and feet have razor-sharp talons. Others say it is more humanlike, only extremely gaunt and emaciated, its head similar to a stag's with antlers. Over the years, stories have been told of people being possessed by a wendigo spirit and committing horrific and gruesome acts. These stories and legends, instead of fading into the mists of time, continue to circulate, and people still claim to encounter wendigos. Additionally, the claims have given rise to a culture-bound disorder known as wendigo psychosis. This is the idea that a person could become a wendigo or that they could be taken over by one. However, this disorder is heavily influenced by local, folk or Indigenous societies. There has been some research into the disorder being an actual psychiatric illness, but for the most part, its authenticity as documented DSM psychosis is disputed among psychologists. So if it isn't a mental psychosis, could it be supernatural? Could someone be taken over by a spirit entity? Some believe they can.

Do mysterious and sometimes malevolent spirits, elementals and creatures really live in the forest? Our ancestors certainly thought so. In ancient times, everyday life and folklore comingled. The belief that a myriad of supernatural beings and spirits inhabited the land, forests, lakes and even homes was very common among our ancestors. Passed down through word of mouth or written accounts, the stories and lore continue to circulate, though often changing to fit the times. It is often said that at their core, folklore and myth have a grain of truth in them. Maybe this is why they still resonate with us. Perhaps, too, the stories endure because the strange creature sightings and encounters with the paranormal endure. In fact, more than one account of encounters with frightening spiritual entities has been reported in the Manistee National Forest. When our ancestors faced a strange beast or spiritual entity in the forest, they probably would have associated it with folklore that was part of their culture, and thus they would have been familiar with what they were encountering. They would have just as likely found a supernatural cause. On the other hand, in our modern world, most people are not as familiar with the majority of the folklore. Furthermore, even if they have heard these tales of old, they believe them to be nothing more than superstition or fiction. Therefore, some of those who claim to have had strange forest encounters do not relate them to these spirits or entities that are believed to have existed for all time. While science has explained many things that would have seemed inexplicable to our ancestors, things exist that science still has no explanation for. Elementals, forest spirits, skinwalkers, Dogman and Bigfoot all reside within the confines of that unknown realm. For the most part, science does not give these accounts any credence whatsoever, so little effort is made to research or explain them other than to chalking them up to imagination, misidentification or a hoax.

Lest you fear that you could be attacked by some unseen spirit or creature while in the Manistee Forest, take heart, as in spite of the dangers that one might encounter in the forest, nature in all its fullness thrives. As you partake of its wonder and beauty, its continuity nourishes the soul and enlivens the mind. Truly, there is peace and healing to be found in nature. This essential goodness is very much evident in the forest. This fundamental life force is present in every tree, shrub, plant or flower that grows. Whether or not you believe that fairies, gnomes, elementals and other mythical woodland creatures reside within its depths, the forest draws us in, and Mother Nature weaves an enchantment around every aspect of our venture. When viewed from a paranormal standpoint, there may indeed be things residing in its depths that we should look on with caution. Indeed, there have been countless documented accounts of strange encounters or events in forests. While it may be good to bear this in mind, it shouldn't deter one from enjoying the forest's beauty. The magic of the woods and its allure stems from its ability to bring a sense of tranquility and peace, things often absence in civilization. This fascination also comes from centuries of the mysticism surrounding the beings that are said to reside in and/or protect the forest. We feel its pull, even for those who do not believe that the forest holds uncanny things.

Let's face it: we like to be scared once in a while. It's why scary books and horror movies are so popular. Whether it's the sense of danger one might feel if they were to go Bigfoot or Dogman hunting or the idea that one could become prey to a skinwalker or a malevolent woodland spirit—there is a certain thrill that goes along with venturing into the forest. Of course, there are pitfalls to avoid when in the forest—most campers and hikers know this—but if the stories of Bigfoot, skinwalkers, ghosts, spirits or elementals can be believed, there are also dangers of the paranormal kind. Even so, one should not get the idea that the forest is only a place filled with frightening creatures, ghosts, or strange entities. In any case, if looked on with reverence and treated with respect, the Manistee National Forest, like any forest, is truly a place of magic and wonder. So the next time you go out hiking, trail riding or just for a leisurely walk in the woods, take a close look around, as you might get a glimpse of something unfamiliar, wondrous or just plain strange hiding behind a tree or a bush. If you're lucky, you just might see the guardian spirit of the woods.

CHAPTER 4
MURDER, MAYHEM AND MADNESS: GHOSTS OF DUDGEON SWAMP

Stopping alongside the road, the ghost hunter grabbed his equipment and headed into the thick brush toward what he believed was the former location of the Dudgeon house. Walking slowly toward a bank of trees, he began to feel an uncanny heaviness in the air and a profound sense of foreboding, like something was telling him that he shouldn't be there. Thinking it was just his imagination, he shook it off and gradually made his way through the thick mud and dry underbrush, although now he was a bit anxious. Warily, he peered into the dense grove of trees. Unexpectedly, he saw a misty haze form up ahead, high up in the branch of a tree. Curious now, he crept closer to get a better look. What he saw horrified him, for swinging slowly from the branch was the shadowy, transparent apparition of a man with a noose around his neck. Then, as quickly as it had appeared, the disturbing image was gone, fading into nothingness. He had heard the stories about the ghost of a murdered man who was said to appear on occasion, but he still was not prepared to actually see it. The murdered man was Romie Hodell, who had been found hanging in a barn on the property many years ago. The ghost hunter was a seasoned paranormal investigator and had experienced some pretty odd things, but coming face to face with the apparition was still unnerving. Heaving a sigh of relief that the apparition was gone, he hastily packed up his gear and sped down the bumpy dirt road as fast as he could. He felt lucky that his car had started. Countless other people who came to the Dudgeon Swamp out of curiosity have had their cars refuse to start or their cell phones quit working until they could manage to get out of the swamp.

Above: "Take a step back in time…White Cloud, Michigan. Where the North begins and pure waters flow." Sesquicentennial announcement panel, July 2023. *Historic panel created by Heritage Presentations. Funded by the White Cloud Downtown Development Authority. Author photo.*

Left: Metal plaque with train, White Cloud. One of the first railway stations in the county was located here. *Heritage Museum of Newaygo County. Author photo.*

While the investigator in this scenario is imaginary, countless real ghost hunters have ventured into Dudgeon Swamp after hearing the strange and sordid tale of the Dudgeon family and Romie "Doc" Hodell. Hodell was the unfortunate man who married into the Dudgeon family and ended up murdered and hanged in a barn one day long, long ago. This is a tale of sordid family rumors, violence, mysterious murders, mayhem and ghosts, both of the white sheet variety as well as the ethereal type. This tragic tale is set in the early 1900s. Given the passage of time and the convoluted nature of the events, it is understandable that there is more than one version of what happened. The exact dates of the timeline are a bit muddled, also. The series of odd events that ultimately cumulated in the mysterious demise of David and Romie Hodell all came about near the town of White Cloud, Michigan. The Dudgeons' saga began in 1905, when Charges Dudgeon traded several homes he owned in Holton, Michigan, for 1,280 acres of land in an area known as Big Bear Swamp near White Cloud. White Cloud, a small community of around 1,700 people, is the county seat of Newaygo County. Located near the banks of the White River, it has become quite popular for its trails and outdoor recreation. With over 4,600 miles of trails nearby, White Cloud has been designated a Trail Town. The town also has several parks that are considerably popular. White Cloud recently reached its 150th birthday, holding a sesquicentennial celebration. Big Bear Swamp is within the Manistee National Forest. The forest itself is vast, stretching out almost a million square miles, although broken up due to the small towns that are located within its borders. Many parts are still relatively wild, where cougars and bears are still occasionally seen. Charles settled there with his wife, Alice, and five children, Herman, Wilmer, Lee, Lola and Meady. They began building a two-story house, but it was never finished. The house they built was little more than a shell, with bare walls covered in newspapers and roughly hewn floors. The outside of the structure was unkempt and crude, with uneven boards covered in tar. However, the family raised livestock and did quite well financially, so well that they were the first people in White Cloud to have an electric truck. Electric vehicles were quite popular around the turn of the century but still quite expensive, so many people did not own one, and they were especially rare in rural areas—so it's possible this may have caused some animosity toward the family. Charles, who made a living from raising livestock, dubbed their new home and land Dudgeon Ranch. Unfortunately, soon after moving, they were seen by townsfolk as being crude and unlikable, with many altercations occurring between the Dudgeons and their neighbors over cattle grazing and property rights. It is said that good fences make good neighbors, but that adage certainly did not work for the Dudgeons. One major sore point was when Charles fenced in his property to keep his cattle from wandering but the fence prevented grazing access for other ranchers. Allowing access to grazing land was something the local ranchers had been doing for years until the Dudgeons came. Angry that their cattle were denied grazing land, they soon took to cutting the fence, letting Dudgeon's cattle out. Needless to say, Dudgeon and his sons were livid. It wasn't long before things came to a head between the Dudgeons and some of the townsfolk. Many of their interactions led to physical violence, and more than once, the Dudgeon boys were charged with assault and ended up in jail.

On the whole, the neighbors' varying views ranged from feeling that the Dudgeons were obstinate and difficult to get along with to being convinced that they were actually insane. Clearly, it didn't help that the Dudgeons seemed to be rather volatile in their dealings with others. The animosity toward the family was in no small part due to the disputes over grazing rights but was possibly also due to a little bit of jealousy on the part of the townsfolk, who may have been rankled that an outsider who seemed to have been quite well off financially came in, bought such a large plot of land and shut them out. Consequently, neighbors fostered a deep dislike and mistrust of the family, and strange rumors soon started to swirl around them. One particularly disturbing and heartbreaking rumor had it that when she was still a teenager, Meady Dudgeon gave birth to two children, fathered by her own brothers. These

"History of White Cloud, Morgan, est. 1873." Sesquicentennial announcement panel, July 2023. *Historic panel created by Heritage Presentations. Funded by the White Cloud Downtown Development Authority. Author photo.*

Stage Door Players Theater, White Cloud, Michigan. *Author photo.*

Historic White Cloud Main Street, 1907. *Postcard. Published by Will P. Canaan, Grand Rapids, for N.L. Lane & Co., White Cloud, Michigan. Public domain.*

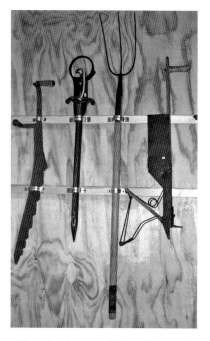

Farm implements. *Heritage Museum of Newaygo County. Author photo.*

babies were taken to the barn soon after being born, and the brothers ruthlessly killed them. This distressing story has never been proven true, and no birth records exist for any such babies. It isn't known who started this horrendous story, but it is quite possible it was someone who hated the Dudgeons. Another bone of contention between some of the neighbors and the Dudgeons was a plot of land that Dudgeon had bought and given to his daughter Lola and her husband, Frank. Unbeknownst to Charge Dudgeon, Frank sold the parcel to their neighbor Jake Terwillegar, who harbored a deep dislike for the Dudgeons. The feelings were mutual. It wasn't long before the Dudgeons were getting sent to jail for fighting with Terwillegar, including Alice Dudgeon, who was said to have broken several of Terwillegar's ribs in a fight.

Originally from Ensly Township, near Grant, Romie had come to the White Cloud area to find work as a stumper, a person who removes tree stumps, which was backbreaking but vital work at the time. After most of the trees around White Cloud had been felled during the logging frenzy, much of the surrounding land was left with thousands of large, obtrusive stumps jutting up from the ground. At one time, there were so many of the unsightly eyesores that White Cloud was called "stumpland." The ground was useless for farmland until the stumps were removed; thus, farmers would hire stumpers to remove them. As bad luck would have it, after finding stumping difficult in Grant, Romie found work clearing stumps from the Dudgeons' land. This was where he met and fell in love with Meady Dudgeon. In April 1921, Romie, age twenty-six, and Meady, nineteen, got married, setting in motion a series of events that would have the town as well as the country reeling. The marriage was rocky from the start. Romie was said to have been an extremely jealous man, accusing his wife of infidelity more than once. About a year after Romie married Meady, Romie's elderly father, David Hodell, came to live with the couple, as he was having marital troubles of his own. David had some health issues, and it seemed that Meady found him tiresome and a lot of work. Within a month after moving in with the couple, David Hodell was dead, rumored to have been poisoned by Meady. Unfortunately, it wasn't too long after his father's death that Romie Hodell would meet the same fate; he was found hanging in the barn. While it appeared to have been suicide, there were many suspicious circumstances surrounding the death, and the police soon got involved.

Meady; her mother, Alice; and her brothers were arrested and put on trial for the murders of David and Romie Hodell, but things were still murky. The police investigation and trial dragged on, with much speculation and widespread news coverage. Meady was put on trial for the murder of her father-in-law and as an accessory to murder in her husband's death. Alice was accused of murdering her son-in-law. The brothers were, at various points, accused of either murdering Romie, or having a hand in covering up the murder by trying to make it look like suicide. At one point, the brothers were confronted by a mob who attempted to make them confess by threatening to hang them both. With all the rumors buzzing around, David Hodell's body was exhumed. The body was said to contain enough strychnine to kill a dozen men, although this finding was later disputed. Meady also confessed under questioning to having put strychnine in her husband's coffee, although she later recanted her confession. Her mother, Alice, confessed to having clubbed him in the head to complete the job when the strychnine didn't kill him. Both confessions were elicited after the women were tricked by several policemen dressed as ghosts. The police got this idea after hearing Alice Meady say ghosts were haunting her while she was in jail. Alice and Meady also confessed to having written the three suicide notes that were found, although these were later said to be genuine. This was no cut-and-dried murder case, and the investigations and trials of Meady, Alice, Lee and Herman dragged on into the late 1920s. With its lurid details and countess strange twists and turns, the trial played out on a national level like a paperback novel, and the public ate it up. It had everything: vigilante justice, jealous rivalries, murder, mystery and plenty of ghosts.

Alice, Meady and Lee all believed they were being haunted by the ghosts of David and Romie Hodell as well as Charles Dudgeon. Charles had died in 1920, the year before Meady and Romie were married. The question was: Were they being haunted by "real" ghosts, or were they of the Halloween trick-or-treating variety? Alice and Meady both said they were bothered by the spirits of Charles Dudgeon, David and Romie. Alice said she was being haunted while in jail awaiting trial. However, Lee was being haunted well before David and Romie's deaths. Soon after his father died, Lee claimed to have seen his ghost while working out in the fields. After the trial, it was learned that the Dudgeons had been "haunted" by several policemen in order to extract their confessions, who donned white sheets and pretended to be ghosts. The highly unusual interrogation and rather unscrupulous method worked. Alice and Meady confessed, although eventually, Alice's conviction was overturned. Meady was not able to file an appeal, due to missing the deadline for filing, and ultimately served twenty-seven years in prison, all the while maintaining her innocence. Her brothers, Lee and Herman Dudgeon, each served time in prison for their part in Romie's murder. They had also been interrogated using the "ghost" method. The idea of dressing up as ghosts to force confessions was outlandish and maybe even comical, but clearly, the Dudgeons were experiencing something out of the ordinary. Something terrified them so much that when the police donned sheets and pretended they were the ghosts of David and Romie, they believed it. If you accept as true that the spirits of the dead sometimes try to communicate with the living, especially when they die tragically, then maybe Romie's spirit did appear to Lee, Alice and Meady, perhaps to try and tell them something. However, something else could have been frightening them, something paranormal about the swamp itself.

If spiritual energy left by tragic or emotional events can be imprinted, then perhaps the turmoil and violence that happened at Dudgeon Swamp left an impression on the landscape, maybe even haunting it. A hundred years have gone by, and little remains of the ramshackle house and barn in Dudgeon Swamp where Romie Hodell met his fate. The ruins are difficult to find, but curious people do seek them out. Adventurous folks who dare to venture into the area where GPS and cell phones are useless have also been known to experience problems with their vehicles. While some discount any notion that the swamp is haunted, locals tend to steer clear of the place. Still, those who manage to find the place where the buildings once stood have reported seeing an apparition of a man hanging from a tree limb as well as the apparitions of a man and a woman dressed in 1920s clothing. Others have reported seeing eerie red eyes peering at them, as well as glowing orbs floating in the pitch-black forest. Disembodied voices or other strange noises are said to emanate out of nowhere. When someone dies, we hope that they rest in peace. This is a common sentiment long written on tombstones. Perhaps that sentiment derives from the idea that ghosts can be restless. Spirits have been known to be especially restless if the manner of their death is tragic or if they died under mysterious circumstances.

Being murdered might make a ghost quite restless. David and Romie certainly didn't get any rest after they passed. Their bodies, buried in Goodwell Cemetery, were dug up, not once but twice, for autopsies. Once, suspecting a setup by the police, the Dudgeon brothers went to the grave site to dig up Romie's body themselves. While David's death was ruled murder by strychnine poisoning, there was some evidence that he, in fact, died of a stroke. Romie's death, however, was violent and mysterious. There was as much mystery about how his body was found as there was about what actually killed him. For starters, he was dead before he was hanged in the barn, and even though he supposedly was given strychnine, he appeared to have been beaten. So maybe it is best that we not attempt to brush off lightly these tales of apparitions, ghostly orbs or disembodied voices that echo through the mist-cloaked swamp. Romie's restless spirit may very well wander over this long-forgotten and desolate swamp seeking solace, if one believes in ghosts. Imaginably, Romie's spirit is restless because his murder goes unsolved. However, the Dudgeons were said to be "mad," so perhaps there was something else at play to create such turmoil, animosity and mayhem for the family. Perhaps it was the swamp itself. Indeed, the swamp has long been reputed to be extraordinarily eerie. What if, after entering into the domain of things unknown or malevolent, a kind of madness took hold of them, making them act in heinous ways? Such an idea is highly implausible. Even so, one might want to take the townsfolk's warnings to heart, lest it be true. However, if you do dare to venture into the Dudgeon Swamp, beware, and don't stay long. For the swamp may be lying in wait— to drive *you* mad.

CHAPTER 5

MYSTERIOUS GIRL IN BLACK: GOTHIC GHOST OF THE TRAILS

Sighing with relief, the girl pulled the small cassette player and headphones out of her backpack. It was a crisp autumn day, and the leaves had just started to turn vibrant shades of orange, gold and yellow. The sun was shining, and there was not a cloud in the sky. It was way too nice to be sitting in a stuffy lunch room waiting for her next class to begin, so she headed to her usual spot on the trails behind the school. There, in the peace and quiet, she could listen to some music or read the latest gothic novel. As she sat down, she looked wistfully back toward the school. She liked being by herself for the most part, but it would be nice if she had a friend to talk with sometimes. Still, she had gotten used to be alone and would often keep herself company by reading or listening to her favorite punk rock bands. She was only sixteen, but for as long as she could remember, she couldn't fit in with her peers. That's why when she discovered punk rock bands and their style of dress, she felt it was made for her. The spiked hair, chains and black clothes seemed to speak to her. Soon, wearing black clothes, chain jewelry, spiked black hair, black lipstick and mascara became who she was: a goth. Unfortunately, though, it made others shy away from her, so she secluded herself even more. She found a soft, grassy spot under a tree, sat down and snapped the cassette tape into the player. She looked around to make sure no one else was around but didn't see anyone.

They weren't supposed to bring cassette players or boom boxes to school, and she didn't want hers to be taken away. She knew that being seen wasn't very likely, as this area was pretty secluded. Even though it was close to

Trail at Riverfront Park, Newaygo. The area is well known for its miles of trails. *Author photo.*

the school, this area was covered with a thick grove of trees. Besides, she thought, no one had paid any attention to her when she left. With the cassette player on her lap, she plugged the headphones into the jack and put them on, taking care not to mess up her hair. Turning the volume up as far as it would go, she leaned her head back against the tree and closed her eyes, listening, spellbound, to the music. After a minute or two, she was feeling drowsy, and the device slipped out of her hand and dropped on the ground next to her. Without opening her eyes, she felt around on the ground for it. Suddenly, she felt a stabbing pain in the back of her hand. Bolting upright, she looked down, just in time to see the still-coiled rattlesnake removing his fangs from her hand, which now had two bloody punctures in it. Terrified and panicking, she scrambled to her feet, tore off her headphones and ran toward the school. Her heart pounded wildly as the venom coursed through her body and her organs started to fail. She desperately tried to make it to the school to get help, but the toxin worked too quickly. She fell to the ground, dying on the spot. Her body is said to have lain there for quite some time before anyone discovered it, but it was eventually found. Legend has it that ever since that time, the goth girl's shadowy ghost sometimes appears to people who walk on the trail, watching them from a distance. She leans against a tree, looking doleful and sad. She is dressed completely in black.

For at least sixty years, this tragic story of an unknown girl in black whose ghost haunts a wooded area near Newaygo High School has made the rounds. The first telling of this story is believed to date to the early sixties, right after the school was built. The story was a lot simpler then but, over time, has become more detailed and elaborate. According to the sixties version, the girl walked out of a back entrance of the school and was immediately bitten by a massasauga rattler. Research into the area makes this part of the story seem somewhat unlikely, as that section of the building was not built until later on. However, although the details have changed over time, the story has consistently held that she died on the spot and no one found her until quite some time later. Eventually, the tale took on iconic status, becoming a popular local urban legend, one likely heard by more than a few students over the years. The trails run behind the school and are a favorite gathering spot for teens. While this story has changed somewhat over the years, becoming more elaborate over time, the description of the girl does not seem to have changed. She is described as pretty and dressed in a sixties or eighties punk rocker black leather jacket and wearing black boots. She is usually seen in approximately the same part of the trail. She has been alternatively described as looking sad, dispassionate or annoyed when encountered. As far as can be determined, no one that fit this description ever attended the school.

This story has all the earmarks of an urban legend. While poignant and tragic, it has no real basis in fact and, like the opening passage of this chapter, is a bit of poetic fiction. On the other hand, given that over the years, many people have claimed to have seen this apparition, one has to wonder if there isn't something more to the story. As for her dying by snakebite, that's a possibility, because even though you might not associate Michigan with rattlesnakes, the state indeed has them. While they are not widespread, there are several counties in Michigan with rattlesnake populations, including Newaygo County. Although it is quite rare, people are occasionally bitten. Michigan has only one type of poisonous snake: the massasauga rattler. If you seek to enjoy the Michigan outdoors, snakes might not be uppermost in your mind, so it might come as a surprise that along with its positive attributes, Michigan has eighteen types of snakes of various sizes and levels of dangerousness. Most of these are not dangerous, of course, although some may act aggressive if threatened. Several species, such as the northern water snake, eastern hognose and blue racer, do resemble or act like their poisonous counterparts, leading people to mistake them for deadly species. Rattlesnakes conjure up visions of dry, arid regions with cacti and cows instead of the lush green foliage and pine trees of Michigan's forests.

The state reportedly has an average of sixteen people a year bitten by the massasauga. Fortunately, though, because of prompt medical treatment, it is rare that people die. Similar to other members of the rattlesnake family, a bite from the massasauga's fangs carries toxic hemolytic venom. The hemotoxin acts to break down and destroy red blood cells in the victim's body, which further affects tissue and organs by breaking down cells and tissue. If an animal or person is bitten, this tissue breakdown will cause immediate pain at the wound site. This venom can either cause the blood to clot or prevent it from clotting, but in any event, the effect on the body can be devastating, causing internal bleeding, cardiovascular failure or the loss of the affected extremity. One major factor in survival is that hemotoxic venom is slower-acting than other forms of venom, giving people time to get medical treatment. Massasaugas are not typically very large, ranging from two to two and a half feet in length with a rattle at the end of their tails that they shake when threatened. However, they are not deemed an aggressive snake and usually prefer to get away from humans. Their skin coloring is gray, tan or brown with black or brown splotches.

Many people fear snakes, and the eastern massasauga rattler is one that you wouldn't want to come across. However, the likelihood that you would find one is slim, as their range is becoming smaller. They are considered threatened and are becoming quite rare in Michigan, although Michigan does have a larger population of the eastern massasauga than other states. You're most likely to see one near water, as their natural habitat is wetlands.

If you are someone who doesn't care for snakes, you might think having fewer snakes is a good thing. On the contrary, they are an important part of the ecosystem, as they assist in keeping down the rodent population. Due to the dwindling massasauga population, efforts are currently being undertaken by a group of conservation partners and contributors from around the state—including the U.S. Forest Service Huron-Manistee National Forest and the Department of Natural resources, among others—to draft the *Michigan Recovery Implementation Strategy for Eastern Massasauga*. This document proposes a five-year goal of improving conservation as well as understanding of the genetic and ecological diversity of the state to facilitate massasauga population growth. Newaygo County is included in that program, along with other counties where the massasauga population is low.

In addition to being an essential part of the ecosystem, snakes are an important symbol in mythology, religion and literature throughout the world. They have often been associated with evil, the underworld or the home of the dead and hold a far-ranging symbolism. The venom itself holds a certain symbolism. Because it can be both a poison and its antidote, it represents a dual nature. The ancients often depicted a snake eating its own tail, known as an Ouroboros and symbolic of eternity. Snakes' ability to shed their skin was believed to represent renewal and rebirth. Other cultures associated snakes with healing and medicine. This association is very recognizable nowadays as the caduceus, a staff with dual snakes entwined around it, carried by Hermes in Roman mythology, symbolizing peace, and from the mythology of the Greek god Asclepius, the snake handler and healer. Thus, their rank among the things of the underworld has often led to snakes being quite misunderstood. The fear of snakes is very common; ophidiophobia, or fear of snakes, is one of the most common phobias. Unfortunately, the mythology surrounding them and their misrepresentation as something evil has led to them often being killed.

It is possible a girl could have been bitten by a rattlesnake once upon a time by the school, though we may never be sure. However, massasauga rattlesnake bite records going back to the 1960s do not list anyone fitting that description ever dying in Newaygo County. Moreover, no student's name has ever been associated with the punk rocker goth girl. In fact, it isn't known if such a person ever existed or attended that school. Furthermore, we don't know if massasaugas were ever a problem at the school. The first school in Newaygo was built in the 1800s, pretty much being carved out of the wilderness. Thus, it's possible that an occasional snake made its way onto school property from time to time. At that time, the school sat alone on a

Opposite, top: Velma Matson Upper Elementary School. *Author photo.*

Opposite, bottom: Desk and bell from the original school in the village of Newaygo, once named Volney School. *Heritage Museum of Newaygo County; author photo.*

Above: Stairs to the elementary school, Newaygo, Michigan. *Author photo.*

grass-covered bluff in the village, giving it a glorious view of the valley below and making it quite a prominent feature in the small village. It has been completely remodeled since the early days and is still in use, its majestic clock tower rising high over the landscape. That first school was surrounded by a large yard, and the hill itself was covered with meadows and orchards that obscured a steep wooden staircase leading up from the town below. One has to think this would have been a particularly arduous journey for children in the wintertime. Parents and grandparents alike enjoy telling childhood stories of how difficult their trek was to and from school. One can imagine that many such stories were told of the numerous stairs students had to climb to get to that first Newaygo schoolhouse. Understandably, the school system has come a long, long way since then. From that lone school on the hill, Newaygo schools now include an elementary, middle and high school with a current enrollment of 1,500 students. There are ninety professionals and fifty support staff employed in the district. According to the Newaygo Schools website, their core values are excellence, responsibility, integrity, respect, safety and compassion, with a successful model that serves to help students explore interests, grasp opportunities for advancement and achieve their full potential.

With the tragic nature of this mysterious ghost—she dresses in black, appears sad, is an outcast and dies tragically by poisoning—the story has all the elements of a Gothic legend. The Gothic genre and its evolving subcultures arose from Victorian-era Gothic novels. These popular novels usually incorporated dark, paranormal or foreboding themes, often intertwined with death and romance. During the 1980s, a gothic culture reminiscent of these motifs evolved: wearing all-black clothing, dying one's hair black and embracing things that are mysterious, dark or paranormal. This culture, known as punk rock, most popular during the 1970s and '80s, was best exemplified by punk rock music. This genre embraced elements of these dark themes as well as the idea of being rejected or alienated from the rest of society. Punk culture was also typified by the themes of darkness, death and alienation but was more rebellious than the more mystical Gothic culture preceding it. Gothic and sub-Gothic themes are still very popular today, with one very popular offshoot being steampunk.

Most assuredly, the dark themes surrounding this rumored ghost has made for an enthralling Gothic legend, one that has stood the test of time locally. Over the years, the punk rocker goth girl has become a popular local urban legend, likely heard by many people in Newaygo through the years in one form or another. It is also likely to be familiar to students today, even though it has been upward of forty to sixty years since she supposedly met her death and returned as a ghost. While it is entirely possible that it is just a story, perhaps there is a core of truth to it. If indeed she was a real person before meeting her untimely death, we may never know who she was or where she came from. If her spirit is haunting the trail, perhaps it stems from a time long before the school was built, or perhaps it is another type of spirit energy. In any case, the punk rocker legend likely resonates with many teenagers or people who feel they are different or outsiders, possibly contributing to its circulation. They might see in this story the same angst they themselves deal with. Skeptics might say the ghost girl accounts and stories are complete nonsense. On the other hand, if one takes the story at face value, one must wonder if there isn't something more to it. Some people believe they see something there lurking along the trail near the school, something dark, foreboding and mysterious. Maybe it is the ghost of a punk rock girl, maybe not. We may never know for sure. We do know that as a ghost, the mysterious punk rocker girl is much like she was in life: dark, mysterious, a loner, always staying apart from others. Like the snake that ended her life, she exists as a symbol of the veil between the living and the spirit world: the place where she finally fit in.

CHAPTER 6

SCREAMING ETHEL: GHOST OF WHISKEY WOOD HILL (JOHN F. WOODS HOUSE)

Imagine walking along River Road in Newaygo. The road is quite narrow and winding. It is a crisp autumn night and almost Halloween. Whiskey Wood Hill is covered with a blanket of gold and crimson leaves. The area, just off State Street, is somewhat remote, and the houses are few and far between. Near the very top of the hill, almost obscured by a towering canopy of trees, you see what is rumored to be a haunted house. As you get closer to this aging and neglected brick house, an unearthly scream pierces the night. A chill runs down your spine. The sound reverberates through the trees from somewhere near or from inside the house, startling you. *Who or what is screaming?* you might wonder as you run away as fast as you can. Hearing a scream under any circumstances would be unnerving. Hearing a scream coming from a house in which no one lives would be more than terrifying; it would be uncanny. But according to local legend, someone or something can be heard screaming near or on Whiskey Wood Hill from time to time. Some say this is the ghost called Screaming Ethel. But how this uncanny screaming ever became attributed to an unknown woman named Ethel is a puzzle, because upon digging into the history of the house, no one named Ethel is immediately clear. The screams are rumored to come from within the house; however, the house has been vacant for many, many years.

There are many strange stories about someone or something called Screaming Ethel and the area known as Whiskey Wood Hill. Some of the stories are rather fragmented and vague. It isn't known how long they have been around or how they got started, but they have evolved into urban

The top of Whiskey Wood Hill from Riverside Drive. *Author photo.*

legends. One story says that a woman hanged herself from a stairway baluster and perhaps her name was Ethel. Another story has it that a man used to bring young women there, whom he later killed. Maybe one of these unfortunate women was named Ethel. While the numerous Screaming Ethel stories that have circulated over the years are spine-tingling and mysterious, the idea that these unearthly screams can be attributed to a ghost named Ethel doesn't appear to have much evidence to back it up, as it seems likely that no one named Ethel was ever associated with the house. However, the complete history of Whiskey Wood House as well as everyone who ever lived there is rather murky. Another tale says a whiskey-loving old man once lived there who rolled his empty bottles down the hill, giving rise to the hill being named Whiskey Wood Hill. Most of the stories connect Screaming Ethel with the house on the hill. Unfortunately, one of the local myths that had been circulating led to some vandalism, prompting the owners to take measures to secure the property and the house. The secrecy surrounding it has resulted in a lot of wild rumors and questions about why it has stayed vacant for so long. Throughout the years, the house has piqued the curiosity of many, including those interested in ghost tales. One of the more ghoulish rumors suggested that perhaps there is a body, or bodies, buried in the basement. Could someone named Ethel be buried there? We may never know. However, the strange screaming sound is not the only bizarre thing believed to happen on Whiskey Wood Hill. People have also seen orbs and strange lights flitting about near the house or in the trees. A Native American trail that runs near the house has been the site of strange mists and small orbs as well.

I was quite intrigued by the house that has come to be known as Whiskey Wood Hill House, both by its history and the story of Screaming Ethel. During a research trip, I had the opportunity to visit the site after participating in a ghost story forum/discussion at Flying Bear Books and Creperie. The small group shared both their own stories and a wealth of fascinating information and details about the town, as well as some of the resident ghost stories and legends, Screaming Ethel included. At the forum, I discovered that Whiskey Wood Hill was right down the road from Flying Bear Books and Creperie. Since it was still light out and a nice day, I decided to go check it out on my way back home. After going about a mile, I didn't see the house, so I turned around and headed back to the main road. On the way back down the hill, I saw it amid the thick brush and trees on the top of a very steep hill, standing like a fortress keeping watch over the landscape. The windows are boarded up, and it stood like a lonely sentinel, desolate and bleak. It was quite obvious that no one has lived in the house for many years. I couldn't get a close look at the house, as "No trespassing" signs are posted on property due to the vandalism. However, I did make out the remnants of an iron fence, its gate sagging and a chain barring entry, across the overgrown driveway.

The property overlooks Newaygo as well as the Muskegon River. The house and property go back to the very early days of Newaygo and feature very prominently in its history. The house was built by John F. Woods after he bought 250 acres of land. Woods, originally from New York State, settled in Newaygo in 1857. John was ambitious, and as a young man, he worked at his father's farm during the summer months and attended school in Moriah, New York. His first wife, Amelia, whom he married in Rouse Point, New York, died after only one year of marriage. He then married Elizabeth Walker in 1864. He and Elizabeth had three children: Isabel, Charles and John F. In Newaygo, Woods took up farming and worked in the lumber industry, buying forest land for the production of lumber. At one time, he was part owner of Grave's Store. He subsequently leased the Brooks sawmill, which John Brooks had built in 1843 along the mouth of Brooks Creek.

John F. Woods House (a.k.a. Whiskey Wood Hill House). *Author photo.*

Woods was a prominent Newaygo citizen, having served at various times as sheriff as well as church deacon. He was passionate about temperance reform, becoming very active in promoting abstinence. Some may have found his stance too rigid and started to poke fun at him. Apparently, this led to the stories of the whiskey bottles being rolled down the hill, and the name Whiskey Wood Hill has been associated with the property ever since. Tragically, in 1888, Mr. Woods was struck by a train and sustained severe injuries. He died several days later at his home.

The property is currently in private ownership. Offers have been made to purchase it, but the owners do not want to sell. Although it remains vacant, someone does maintain the property, cutting the grass when needed. They have also installed outside lights to deter vandals and curiosity seekers. The house, made of brick, has deteriorated somewhat over the ensuing years, but its overall appearance has weathered those years relatively well. With

John F. Woods House (a.k.a. Whiskey Wood Hill House), Newaygo, April 6, 2015. *By rossograph, own work, CC BY-SA 4.0. Wikimedia Commons.*

all the mystery and ghost stories surrounding the house, interest in it has, understandably, grown. From a paranormal perspective, its abandoned appearance and isolated wooded surroundings may be enhancing the house's mystique. When you intertwine this with strange scream-like noises, orbs and mists, it is not surprising that it has become of interest to paranormal investigators.

Nevertheless, from a historical perspective, the house on Whiskey Wood Hill deserves respect and consideration in the vital part it played in the building of Newaygo. While the stories have undoubtedly been embellished over time, the numerous accounts of orbs, strange lights and unearthly screams experienced nearby shouldn't be disregarded entirely. Orbs, mists and discarnate sounds are often associated with the paranormal or spirit world. Orbs are transparent balls of light that some believe are spiritual in nature, being either ghosts or guardian angels or other otherworldly phenomena. They have been seen with the naked eye and photographed in a variety of locations, both indoors and out, but are said to be most prominent in suspected haunted places, crop circles, burial grounds or cemeteries. They are described as being of various sizes, shapes and colors. Numerous photographs have captured these curious, elusive balls of light, although some regard them as simply dust particles or moisture on their camera lens. At any rate, orbs have become a prominent feature in paranormal investigation in recent years. While some sightings and photographic evidence may be discounted as photographic anomalies or misidentification, there have been other reliable reports and photos that would indicate that some form of energy is responsible for orb manifestation. Whether or not orbs are proof of the existence of ghosts has yet to be discovered.

However, the "screams" could also have a very real source. The house is surrounded by forestland, so it's home to many woodland creatures, including owls. In fact, Michigan is home to eleven different species of owls, three of which have vocalizations that may be frightening when one is not familiar with them. The great horned owl has many different calls, many of which sound ominous and strange. Their range covers the Americas, and they stay in Michigan year-round. Likewise, the shrill screech of the barn owl is so strange they have been called ghost owls, demon owls or death owls. The remarkable calls of the long-eared owl are varied, including grumbling, cackling and cat-like screams, and they can be heard from a great distance. Thus, if one is not familiar with their strange, unearthly calls, they might give you quite a fright, even in the light of day. So, if you ever happen to go near Whiskey Wood Hill in the dead of night, see eerie red lights flickering atop the hill and hear the blood-curdling scream of "Ethel," have no fear. It is only the shriek of an owl—isn't it?

CHAPTER 7

A PIONEERING SPIRIT:
THE KINDLY GHOST OF
DOCTOR QUICK

For many years, it has been said that late in the evening, along River Drive in Newaygo, a phantom-like light can be seen in the distance, flickering through the thick blanket of trees that covers a hillside near the Muskegon River. The source of this inexplicable light is unknown, but it has been seen by locals for a number of years. Perhaps this spectral light is a phantasm of something that no longer exists: the lantern that once hung in the window of a humble cottage now crumbled to the ground. It is also said that the ghostly figure of an elderly woman, dressed in modest clothing, her gray hair pulled back into a bun is seen gliding across the green grassland and brush before disappearing. She seems to be searching as she wanders over the hill, sometimes stooping as if she is picking up something. If the stories are to be believed, this would be the ghost of Dr. Florence Quick. Florence was a popular and beloved folk medicine doctor who once lived and worked her medicine in the Newaygo area, not far from Whiskey Wood Hill and Riverfront Park. Some people say her ghost still lives on the hill.

If any story symbolizes the rugged life of the early Newaygo pioneers, it is the heartrending yet inspirational story of Dr. Florence Molonson Quick. Florence was born on August 5, 1828, near St. Johns, Canada. Her parents, Leona (Tait) and Joseph Molonson, were from France. It is known that she had a good relationship with the Native Americans living in the area and learned much from them about the use of herbal medicine and ways of living harmoniously with nature. Using this knowledge, she became well-known among the locals for her herbal remedies. Florence was described as

Whiskey Wood Hill. *Author photo.*

Swampy area at Riverfront Park, Newaygo. *Author photo.*

a loner, strong and independent yet kind and compassionate, and was always willing to help the less fortunate. Perhaps this was because of the hardships she herself had endured. These hardships started early on. Florence was only two years old when her mother died. After her mother's death, her father took Florence and her brother Moses to Detroit and then to Grand Rapids, before finding work in the lumber trade near Mill Creek. At that time, Grand Rapids was little more than a small trading post. He then decided to make his way back to Canada to secure funds, taking off on foot. Unfortunately, he left Florence and her brother alone in a small shanty with few provisions. Florence was five, and Moses was seven. Their father had enlisted some of his friends in Grand Rapids to look after them. Regrettably, these friends soon forgot about the two young children entrusted to their care, and Florence and her brother were left to their own devices. Joseph had only planned on being gone for a month but contracted typhoid, so he was unable to travel. He did not return for the children for an entire year.

Their meager provisions having quickly run dry, Florence and Moses subsisted by foraging for roots, bark and berries. Providentially for the children, a French trader by the name of Magalpin was accompanying a large group of Native Americans to Grand Rapids. They made camp for the night near the shanty and began preparing an evening meal of venison, bread and ground corn. All the while, the starving children watched the group through cracks in the shanty. They had no need to fear, as the women of the group soon took them under their care. The children were given food, bundled in blankets and taken along to Grand Rapids. Following this, they lived with Magalpin and his Native American wife for a time. They were happy living with the Magalpins when Joseph returned with his new wife. Things did not go well for Florence after that, and she left home. She was only eight years old when she went to work for a Detroit family, working there for four years. Later, she went to live with her sister in Grand Haven for a short time. She then moved to Muskegon. In Muskegon, she began working for the lumber baron Martin Ryerson and his family. Another sister, living in Croton at the time, sent word to Florence, inviting her to visit. Florence made her way there as best she could. She, along with some Native American friends, traveled up to Croton by canoe, stopping at the Brooks lumber camp to get provisions. At the time, the lumber camp was the only occupied place in Newaygo. As fortune would have it, the next morning, Mr. Brooks enlisted Thomas Quick and his team to drive Florence the rest of the way to her sister's. Thomas took an obvious shine to Florence, and the feeling was apparently mutual, as she married Thomas three months later.

Florence was fifteen years old. Thomas was thirty-three. Their wedding, held at John Brooks's home, was officiated by two Grand Rapids justices of the peace, who traveled there by horseback. The newlyweds stayed with the Brookses for the winter. In the spring, they took a lumber barge to Chicago to buy furnishings for their new home a bit downriver. Their home was little more than a shanty, yet they had seven children while living there, four of whom died early on. Florence and Thomas were married for eight years before he died.

Given that her early years were spent in the wilderness and, for the most part, on her own, it is unlikely that Florence had any medical knowledge other than home remedies popular at the time. What she learned from her Native American friends was helpful in many aspects. Medicine in the late 1800s was still in its infancy, especially in rural areas. Granted, it had advanced from some of the mediocre and often unfounded medical theories that early colonists had brought with them. Many of those theories went back to the first school of medicine in Europe and had merged with other, earlier beliefs, most notably those of Hippocrates. However, instead of being based on scientific principles, many of these theories and practices were based on myths, beliefs or superstitious rites. Such beliefs spread across Europe and England and eventually to the New World. Accordingly, the practice of medicine in the colonial period was variable and primitive at best. But eventually, interaction between early pioneers and Native inhabitants, changes in theories about disease and the shift to a scientific approach made significant contributions to the progression of medicine in early America.

At one time, medical practitioners were divided into three distinct groups: physicians, surgeons and apothecaries. This division worked well in Europe but was impractical in America. Here, life was hazardous, with disease or sudden death a real possibility, especially since many areas of the United States were still sparsely populated and medical care was not accessible. Additionally, physicians were scarce and had little training, and treatment was rudimentary at best. With no credentials being required to practice, many passed themselves off as doctors. Moreover, even the qualified ones had a limited amount of information and skills. For this reason, many early pioneers used home remedies. Such therapies were an admixture of astrological lore, "grandmother's" remedies and patent medicines. Conversely, Native American views on health and remedies were radically different from those early theories. While there are no written records to mark Native American history before the arrival of Europeans, we do know something of their medicine from written observations of Indian medicine

Buggy owned by Dr. Whitehead, first doctor in Newaygo. *Display at Heritage Museum of Newaygo County. Author photo.*

by early explorers. Native American healers used herbal medicines for conditions such as burns, broken bones and sore eyes, but some of their medicines seemingly cured conditions that had no outward physical cause known at the time. They believed in balance and harmony, with a great reverence for nature and its supernatural powers.

In many Native American cultures, these healers were called shamans. Shamans are those with the ability to work with earth energies, "see" visions and heal. In the Southwest, these medicine workers were known as *curanderos* and *curanderas*. The Algonquin societies also had shamans, known as the midewiwin. The first mention of the midewiwin was in association with the Potawatomi, who lived in the Detroit area in the early 1700s, although their origins likely precede this time frame. Midewiwins were a uniting element between differing communities. While much lore has been passed down involving the manitou, tricksters or sorcerers in Native American mythology, little mention has been made of the midewiwin. The role and healing methods of the shaman varied; oftentimes, they used ceremonies, but some used charms or fetishes as well as medicines derived from plants. The Native Americans had developed a system whereby each medicinal plant or root was assigned to one of the four directions of the compass. This reflected the universal circle of life, energy, influence and relationships and was spiritual in nature. Native Americans knew much about North American plant cures, having no doubt learned by trial and error over the centuries of inhabiting the continent. Although Native American medicine was slow to be widely accepted, some physicians, like Benjamin Rush of Philadelphia, began studying Indian herbal medicine in the 1770s. Medicine then became a loosely tied-together framework of traditions and methods, from the practices and methods of the Native Americans to the practices that the early pioneers brought with them across the seas. This kind of transformation takes place in cultures and societies through the interaction of people and relationships and gradually changes the conditions under which these relationships take place. Thus, it seems that Dr. Florence Quick, in her use of Native American herbs and remedies, was an innovator.

Florence lived in that simple one-story shanty near the river for more than forty-five years. Although she kept to herself for the most part, she would often be seen out in the fields, picking herbs, mushrooms or wildflowers. Her life was difficult and fraught with hardship, but she didn't let that prevent her from helping others. She continued to be kind and compassionate to others, feeding the hungry, taking care of them when they were sick and taking in those who had nowhere to go. Perhaps this is because she knew what it was like to go without and did not wish it for others. Many times, she had no way to support herself and looked to the kindness of friends to help with food and fuel, but what she had, she shared. Later on, she sold her property to the Newaygo Portland Cement

Company and received a pension as compensation. Many years have passed since the time of Florence Quick, and she is no longer of this earth, yet some say she can still be seen wandering the hillside near the Muskegon River. Imaginably, her spirit is still roaming the woodlands in search of healing herbs, still doctoring from the beyond, with the light from her shanty beckoning all those who seek healing and comfort.

CHAPTER 8
STRANGE VISITOR: HOWLING HELLHOUND

About thirty years ago, my then-husband and I were visiting with our friends John and Sandy at their cabin in White Cloud, very close to the Manistee Forest. There was a fence running alongside the cabin. Being so near the forest, there were a lot of densely wooded spots nearby. The men had spent most of the day hunting, and it was quite late when they arrived back. Sandy and I had spent the day browsing antique shops and catching up. It had been a full day, and we were all exhausted, so after we had a quick dinner, chatted and played a few hands of rummy, we all retired for the night. The cabin had two bedrooms, and the bedroom where my husband and I were to sleep had a small window that overlooked the fence and the woods beyond. After I fell into a deep sleep, a nightmare jarred me awake. In the dream, a large, menacing black dog was chasing me, its teeth bared. I woke up and looked at the clock. It was almost midnight. Still half asleep, the nightmare still upon me, I peered cautiously around the darkened bedroom, heart pounding, to make sure there was nothing in the room with me. I was mystified; it seemed so real. Obviously, there was no dog in the room. Relieved that it was just a dream, I went back to sleep. I'm not sure how long I was asleep, but I was again jolted out of my sleep, by an eerie howl. This time, it was not a dream. Again, something howled. This unnerved me, and I was still unsettled from the nightmare, but I was curious, so I got up to see what the strange howling was about. I pulled back the curtain and looked out the window. Peering into the darkened yard, I could just make out the shape of a very large black dog sitting beyond the fence, looking toward the cabin. When it saw the curtain move, it seemed to look toward me, its eyes glinting red. For the third time, it howled. Then, inexplicably, it seemed to disappear into the dark. Panic-stricken, I hurriedly closed the curtains and went to wake my husband, to no avail. My husband was a very sound sleeper, and he never budged as all of this was going on. I went back to bed and tried to get some sleep. It was three o'clock in the morning. Thankfully, there was no more howling heard that night. At breakfast, I told my husband and our friends about my strange visitor the previous night. They laughed it off, as did I, although I couldn't help but shake the feeling that there was something very strange about the incident, that it was a portent of some sort. We packed up, secured everything in the cabin and left right after breakfast. John and Sandy dropped us off at our apartment in Ravenna and then headed home. That evening, Sandy called me and told me that her father had passed away suddenly in the middle of the night. Sometime later, I learned the time of her father's death was three o'clock, the exact time the spectral black dog howled for the third and last time.

While my dream and visitation by a strange black dog seemed to be a very bizarre occurrence, seeing or having dreams of spectral black dogs is not all that unusual. In fact, folklore and myths surrounding spectral black dogs have been known for some time throughout Spain, the British Isles, other parts of Europe and the United States. The origin of these myths is difficult to determine, but they possibly derived from Celtic or Germanic cultures and were disseminated through expansion and colonization as people settled in new locations. These terrifying supernatural entities, often associated with the Devil or hellhounds, are said to be unusually large, sometimes as large as a calf, with long teeth, razor-sharp claws and glowing red eyes. In addition to black, they have been described as various other colors: brown, white and even spotted. They are reportedly seen during severe electrical storms and at ancient pathways such as ley lines and places of execution or death. They are also linked to crossroads or fairy mounds in the British Isles. Much of mythology paints them as being malevolent or having sinister intent, and they are most often seen as a portent of death, although in some instances they are regarded as guardians, guides or protectors. At these times, they will warn of danger or death. The Black Dog of Hanging Hills, Connecticut, has all three of these factors woven into its mythology. The first sighting portends a good omen, the second will bring sorrow and the third sighting, death.

In the British Isles, there are certain families where the appearance of the Black Dog is a generational one. Seeing the Black Dog means the death of a family member, similar to the appearance of the banshee. Other folklore relates that just seeing the Black Dog can cause one to die of fright. Other stories common in Scotland regard them as being guardians of secret treasure who do not cause harm to people unless they attempt to steal it. One spectral dog known in Leeds, England, as Padfoot is said to be kindly to those who are kind to it. Some have speculated that the mythical Black Dog originates from the supernatural or otherworldly realm. Thus, they can or will only make themselves known to serve a specific purpose, portend death or warn. Some assert that they perhaps cause harm. One such event was said to have happened in Suffolk, England, in 1577, when the Black Dog was seen during a severe storm. The dog ran into a church and frightened two parishioners who were kneeling in prayer, whereupon they both fell to the ground and died. It then appeared at Blythburgh shortly afterward and was believed to have resulted in three deaths there. To this day, Black Dog sightings continue in and around places that are associated with legends or the paranormal. Some of the names or types of the Black Dog in folklore are hellhound, church grim or spirit. The grim is believed to act as the guardian of a specific church and churchyard, warding off thieves or other malevolent entities. Black Dogs are also theorized to be the spirits of dogs, demons or personifications of the devil, being known as Shuck in many parts of England, meaning "devil" or "fiend."

Did I encounter a hellhound? That is very difficult to say. My nightmare as well as the visitation by a black dog seemed to be of a paranormal nature and were very similar to many aspects of the folklore surrounding the Black Dog, with the exception that they did not appear to be connected with any deaths or disasters happening to my family at the time. However, it could still have been connected to the death of my friend's father, as we were all in the same cabin. The nightmare itself also fits into the realm of the subconscious, collective consciousness, archetypes and the nature of dreams, whereby everything is connected. If one were to assign a ghostly meaning to all of this, perhaps at one time someone who lived near the cabin owned a black dog that died or was buried there, and now its spirit is bound to the site. It seemed a rather uncanny coincidence that my friend's father died the same night and time that I saw the black dog and had the nightmare, given the mythology surrounding such a sighting. To this day, I am not sure what I experienced. A ghost hunter would probably say it was undeniably a ghost dog I saw that night. They might suggest that I should have tried to get it to leave, which seems reasonable when you're dealing with ghosts. One common way a paranormalist would have done this is by gently explaining to the spirit that it is no longer among living and that it is alright for it to "pass over." But this raises the question: how does one get a ghost dog to leave? Does one offer him a treat if he will, or tell him it is OK for him to go play in that yard in the great hereafter? No one knows for sure how it all works. But one thing is for certain: provided he was not a hellhound, even with all the eerie howling waking me up in the middle of the night, he was most definitely a good boy.

CHAPTER 9

THE NIGHT SHIFT: GHOSTS OF OLD GRANT HOSPITAL

It had been a pretty typical evening at the center. Meal trays had been picked up, visitors had gone home and the clients were all safely tucked away for the night. The nurse stood at the counter. She had just finished writing up her notes and was getting ready to count a client's medication before going home. Suddenly someone, or something, whispered in her ear. It was low and guttural, almost growling. Coming from a person, this would have been upsetting enough, but there was no one there, just an ominous voice from out of nowhere. This was all too much for the weary nurse, and she ran screaming in terror down the hallway, much to the shock of her coworkers.

This unnerving story is only one of the many tales that have been told throughout the years of a former hospital in Grant, Michigan. The hospital, built in the 1940s as Grant Community Hospital, was closed in 1983 as St. Mary's Hospital and has been the site of an assisted living center since 1997. Much of the strangeness seemed to happen at night. The elevator doors were said to inexplicably open and close by themselves, and the elevator went up or down without any passengers. People would see fleeting shadows or hear a baby crying. There are no babies at the center, although the area where the crying was heard was formerly a maternity ward. One section of the L-shaped building contained a dementia unit; another section housed a memory care unit. There was also a dining area and a social and activities area. There was a piano in the activities room. One curious incident involved a staff member who was picking up dinner trays from the clients' rooms

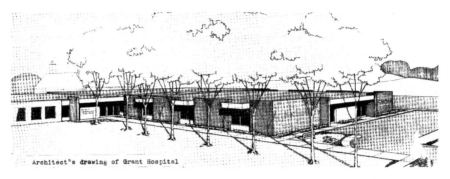

Architect's drawing of Grant Community Hospital. *From* Pictorial History of Grant, Michigan, *White Cloud Library.*

late one night. It was very quiet in the building, as all the clients were in their rooms and sleeping. As the worker walked past the activities room, the piano bench creaked, as if someone was sitting on it. Thinking that one of the clients was up playing the piano, the worker looked into the room and was surprised to find no one there. Another perplexing nighttime event happened when all the clients were all in their rooms and sleeping. A staff member was walking past a client's room when something banged loudly on the client's door from inside their room. This banging was strong enough to jar the decoration that was on hallway side. Thinking that maybe a client had fallen against the door, the staff member went into the room to check. However, the client was sound asleep. Nothing had fallen against the door, and there were no windows open that could have caused a draft.

Adding to the mystery and lore of the former hospital is the rumor that beneath it are tunnels that once led to a funeral home, although this is not substantiated. If that is the case, understandably, it might be a bit unnerving to some. It is said that some staff members did not wish to go into the basement alone for that reason. It is not unheard of for hospitals to have had tunnels beneath them. In fact, many larger institutions in the early days had large tunnel systems and lower levels that contained their electrical power systems or led to storage facilities. Possibly, some of them led to funeral homes. Even now, hospital morgues are usual hidden away in the basement so as to avoid transporting the bodies past patients' rooms, which of course would be upsetting. Before the days of refrigeration, it seems very reasonable that they were located beneath the ground, because the tunnels were cooler. Thus, if there was a tunnel beneath Grant Hospital leading to a funeral home, in all probability it was constructed in the early days of Grant, when it was still a fledging community.

Above: Former Grant
Community Hospital.
Author photo.

Right: Grant, Michigan
businesses. *Author photo.*

Now a flourishing rural community in southern Newaygo County, Grant had its beginnings in 1882 as Grant Center after Andrew Squier built a sawmill in the area. At its inception, it was called Grant Center due to its central location. Located along M-37, it is about six miles from the town of Newaygo and about twenty-five miles away from Grand Rapids and Muskegon. There are about 900 people and 230 families living in and around the area. The first post office was established in 1892 at Grant Station, which became Grant in 1899 after incorporation. Grant was reincorporated as a city in 1962. As was the case with many towns and villages in the county, the lumber industry played a vital part in the village's growth, with sawmills quickly popping up. Shortly after this, Grant Railroad Station was built to serve the burgeoning lumber industry as well as the growing population. At the peak of the lumber era, over a million feet of lumber was shipped out every year. Log trains would transport logs from Grant to Newaygo. The station and town get their name from president and general Ulysses S. Grant. There was a Western Union, a train depot and a large water tower. Constructed of pine and cypress, the tower could hold over forty-two thousand gallons of water. Contributing much to the town's history, the water tower is a prominent feature in Grant and a nationally recognized historic site.

The depot and water tower were constructed as part of the Chicago and West Michigan Railroad system in 1891, eventually becoming part of the Pere Marquette Railway system. From its establishment, Grant Station was vital to the lumbering industry in Newaygo. Much of the lumber that came out of Newaygo's forests went through the station. From 1872 to 1873, a massive 9 million feet of logs were transported. In 1885, sawmill owner and founder Andrew T. Squire was generating 1 million feet of logs a year. Up until the 1940s, Grant Depot served railroad passengers, with two trains making runs between Grand Rapids and Traverse City. After the demise of the lumber industry, like many other towns in the county, Grant turned to agriculture to further its economic growth, and soon the railroad station became a vital part of the town's economy. Although the railroad system met its demise, agriculture has remained important. Visitors to Michigan, especially those traversing the highways and byways of the upper regions, are often delighted to find local produce stands or farmer's markets. In fact, many people take trips in order to seek out farm-fresh produce as well as enjoy places with a small-town feel. Grant is one such place. Each year, the City of Grant holds its Harvest Moon Festival in the downtown area, which focuses on the area's plentiful agricultural wealth. The 2023 celebration

Chittenden grain elevator, near Water Tower Park, Grant, Michigan. *Author photo.*

featured a parade, music and live entertainment, an arts and craft fair, food booths, games, tractor display, a kids' carnival and other events. Grant Farmer's Market, located near the water tower, is regularly sought out for its produce and goods. Vendors sell a variety of fruits, vegetables, plants and flowers as well as baked goods and arts and crafts. In the early years, Grant shipped a large portion of its agricultural produce by rail. Ten to twelve cars of peaches a day were being transported in 1915. Onions were another product regularly shipped out from Grant fields. In the 1930s, so many onions were shipped that Grant became known as the Onion Capital of the World.

After the last passenger train ceased operation in 1963, the water tower continued to be used as a water reserve for the fire department until the late 1980s. The depot was refashioned into a restaurant, which is still in operation today. The city owned the water tower; however, it stood on land owned by CSX Transportation, a freight railroad company, and the city had been paying the lease for many years. Although no longer useful, the depot and water tower remained as testimonies to the vital part they played in Grant's—and Michigan's—history. The water tower is one of the last

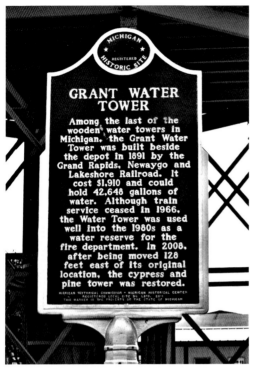

Left: Sign commemorating the Grant water tower as a historic site. Water Tower Park, Grant, Michigan. *Author photo.*

Below: Historic train caboose, Water Tower Park, Grant, Michigan. *Author photo.*

Opposite: Historic water tower. Water Tower Park, Grant, Michigan. *Author photo.*

wooden water towers in the state, and there was interest in having the tower registered as a historical site. In order to do so, it was moved 128 feet to a location by the train caboose. Water Tower Park was moved onto the same site. The historic move attracted many onlookers and even garnered media coverage from local television and newspapers. On June 10, 1980, the tower site was added to the Michigan State Historical Registry. The water tower and the restored original Chessie train caboose are now prominent features of Water Tower Park. The park was constructed with a grant and contributions from the Fremont Area Community Foundation as well as area businesses and residents. In addition to these grand structures, the park has scenic landscaping, picnic tables and benches. In addition to Water Tower Park, there are several other parks where people can enjoy the great outdoors. Blanch Lake Park on Park Drive features an amphitheater, a baseball field, a swimming beach, a boat launch, picnic tables and grills. Dogs are allowed,

provided they are kept on leashes. In recent years, the park, along with local businesses, has hosted movie night events. Fishing is allowed from boats or the dock. For skateboard aficionados, Ryan Benson Memorial Skate Park is located several blocks from M-37.

With its comfortable and welcoming hometown feel, colorful farmer's markets, family-friendly recreation and historic sites, Grant has much to offer as a place to live or visit. While these incidents involving discarnate whispers, strange shadows and loud banging on doors are quite strange, it should be noted that the facility where they are believed to have occurred is a well-established senior living center in the Grant community, has offered high-quality, loving and conscientious care and services to seniors for many years and comes highly recommended. Thus, one should not fear any harm from ghosts at the center. Certainly, no one should be wary of encountering any ghosts there. However, what was it that the staff member heard that sent her screaming down the hallway, and what could have hit a door so hard that it jarred it? We may never know; however, these strange encounters made a lasting impression on those who were said to have experienced them. Some people might say these events were just cases of nerves brought on by rumors or stories. However, it should be noted that nurses and medical personal tend to be the "just the facts" type. Most are not given to hysteria or superstition and, due to their medical schooling, have a keen eye for detail as trained observers. Thus, taken at face value, if there was an unseen guest trying to make their presence known, alarming the nurses in the process, maybe this ghostly trickster is a bit ticked off that they didn't get a dinner tray. Even so, they could try to keep the noise down a little bit. After all, it's the night shift; the nurses have rounds to do, and the clients are trying to sleep.

Chapter 10
Little Fisher Boy: Ghost of Croton Dam

The sun was just coming up. The frail young boy lingered on the narrow strip of cement for a moment, sobbing as he looked down gloomily at the torrents of foaming water rushing through the dam. His hollow eyes were sorrowful, and tears coursed down his cheeks. Precariously, he moved slowly across the top of the dam. His ethereal body, illuminated by the lights, appeared to hover and glide before it descended into the rushing water below, disappearing into the frigid river. Some say this is the ghost of a young boy who was fishing on the top of the dam. Tragically, he slipped and fell into the turbines below. The boy is said to sob as he walks across the top of the dam. Such an event would be terrible if true. However, it may in fact be mere legend. This well-known Newaygo County story has been circulated for some time, possibly dating to the 1970s. Many sightings of this boy are said to happen before the sun rises. Inexplicably, the apparition is sometimes seen hovering about ten feet above the dam wall. Over time, seeing the apparition of the little fisher boy has come to be considered somewhat of a good luck charm by fishermen; it is said that whoever sees him will have good luck that day. If ever a small boy lost his life while fishing on that dam, sadly, no one knows who he was or why he is seen sobbing. If the stories can be believed, perhaps it is because he is doomed to fish forever from the top of the Croton Dam, his cries not heard, his name unknown.

Croton Dam is an embankment dam and power plant on the Muskegon River in Croton Township, a civil township in Newaygo County on the banks of the Muskegon River. The dam, constructed as a means of harnessing the waterpower generated by the river, was a forerunner to Consumers Energy hydroelectric plant. Consumers Energy operates and maintains the Croton Dam along with ten other hydroelectric plants in Michigan. The dam was built in 1907 by brothers William and James Foote under the direction of civil engineer William Fargo. Before building the Croton Dam, William Foote was a gristmill operator who provided power to an electric company from his mill wheel. Intrigued by the potential and viability of using electricity to power streetlights, he founded the Jackson Electric Light Works along with his brother in 1886. They began by lighting streets in Jackson, Michigan, and soon expanded to other cities. Dams were often built to power gristmills and, at times, were refitted to accommodate electric generators, but in some instances new dams were built.

At the turn of the twentieth century, electrical power was most commonly used for streetlights, but with the advent of the streetcar as well as the industrial age, demand grew. With this increased demand came the need for bigger dams. Thus, in 1898, the Foote brothers began working with Fargo on a project that entailed the construction of a trowbridge dam across the Kalamazoo River. With the Muskegon River having the second-greatest discharge of an inland river, Fargo turned his sights to building an earth embankment dam in Croton. Using a newly developed method of construction and contemporary designs, this immense project was completed in a little over three months. Fargo constructed a pumping plant using seven rotary pumps to move the water up a pipeline to a bluff above the Muskegon River. The high-pressure flow of water dispatched the soil and water mixture to iron troughs. This material was then routed back to the dam site. The material was layered as it was deposited and the water allowed to drain off, which compacted the material. This was one of the earliest instances of this technique being used east of the Mississippi River. After the dam was completed in 1907, it garnered a lot of attention and was met with great fanfare. Because the dam employed the latest electric power advances, engineers from around the world came to tour the dam and the powerhouse. In 1931, Croton Dam and Rogers Dam were connected to Hardy Dam, the last large hydroelectric project in Michigan. Rogers, Hardy and Croton Dams are all owned and operated by Consumers Energy. Croton Dam is now considered a historic site and was listed on the National Register of Historic Places in 1979.

The village that thrived around the development of the dam was named Croton after the New York town Croton-on-Hudson. Croton Township was first settled as Muskegon Forks in 1840 and became a village in 1870.

Consumers Energy hydroelectric plant. Croton, Michigan. *AVERY Color Postcard. Anscochrome. By Hoyt Louis Avery. Published by AVERY Color Studios, Saranac, Michigan. Used with permission.*

Riverview is a small unincorporated community within the township. As of the 2000 census, about 3,040 people resided in and around the Croton area. Croton is a serene, picturesque place, revered as a quiet getaway for both locals and visitors, especially in the summer months. It is often referred to as "Michigan's secret paradise" as well as being the "Party Capital" of mid-Michigan. Croton Pond is an artificial lake created between Croton and Hardy Dams, located off Croton-Hardy Drive. People can access the site at the south end of the pond off Croton Drive. The pond has become a popular outdoor recreation spot where people can kayak, fish, camp and swim. Moreover, it is also home to world-class boating and sports fishing and admired for its beautiful natural landscape. A large variety of fish species, including bluegill, bass, pike, walleye, perch and crappie, inhabit the lake. Croton Pond has become a focal point for anyone who enjoys getting out in nature and outdoor activities, whether it's swimming, kayaking, fishing or just enjoying the beautiful scenery and wildlife. There are numerous parks, recreation centers and campsites near the lake as well as a beach area with boat launches, playgrounds, a picnic area and three pavilions nearby. At the southern end of Croton Pond lies Conkin Park, covering twelve acres with a wide variety of recreational facilities, including a baseball field, two tennis courts, a shuffleboard/basketball platform, a disk golf course and a playground. Conklin Park leads to Croton Dam, and a walkway affords easy access to the Muskegon River.

For those who love water-based recreation, Croton seems to have it all, as in addition to the plentiful outdoor recreation opportunities to be had at Croton Pond, there are also plenty of exciting water-based events that take place, especially in the summer months. One such event is the Power Paddle Race that takes place every year. This event is conducted by the Michigan Canoe Racing Association in partnership with the Newaygo Nationals Association. One of the goals of the Newaygo Nationals Association is to bring awareness to the Muskegon River and the watershed, as well as to encourage participation in amateur outdoor recreation and river paddling. The development of these events and competitions is beneficial to helping bring awareness to the river valley. The two-day Power Paddle Race, with cash prizes, happens every year in June. Headquarters of the Newaygo Nationals Association are located at Croton Pond Boat Launch in the DuChemin Park Pavilion on Washington Street. The hardiness of Newaygo County folk is evident when they are enjoying the outdoors: the recreation doesn't stop at the river when the weather turns cold and everything freezes over. In fact, their yearly ice-fishing tournament is a vital part of the area's culture. This fundraiser tournament is held on free-fishing weekend in February, when people can take advantage of the Department of Natural Resources suspending fishing license requirements for the weekend. The proceeds of this tournament go toward a local nonprofit.

There is little to match the beauty and peacefulness of a pristine blue lake or shimmering river or being outside in the sunshine and fresh air, so it is no wonder that people are drawn to nature and bodies of water. Similarly, water also draws in the spirit world, perhaps even holding onto spirits. There are stories about ghosts or apparitions spending their afterlife tied to a watery grave. We don't hear them as often as stories that take place on dry land, so it may come as a surprise to some that spirits are also seen in and around water. Historically, cultural beliefs of some peoples held that because water was capable of removing curses from objects, spirits could not exist beneath the water. However, this does not appear to be the case, according to some paranormal researchers. The idea that a ghost can haunt the watery depths of a lake, river or stream lends a degree of the macabre rarely matched by any landlocked ghost story, especially if you can envision seeing hollow spectral eyes peering up at you from the murky depths.

Right: Vintage swimsuit display, Newaygo, Michigan. The area has been a popular recreation site for many years. *Heritage Museum of Newaygo County. Author photo.*

Below: "View on Muskegon River" postcard, circa 1912. Sent from the Past series. *For S.H. Knox & Co., (F.W. Woolworth & Co.) postmarked 1912. Public domain.*

View on Muskegon River, Muskegon, Mich.

However unsettling that idea is, the spirits of the dead are not the only spirits believed to haunt bodies of water. In fact, there are many other spirits or entities believed to be tied to bodies of water. Some of these spirits are part of tribal lore or other cultural myths. One such entity is a water sprite. While they are similar to ghosts, water sprites are not spirits of the deceased and tend to be grouped in with faeries or elementals. Some of the most well-known water sprites include the banshees believed to inhabit the bogs of Ireland, whose wailing is said to signal the death of a family member. In the United Kingdom, seas, lakes, rivers, streams, ponds and puddles could be home to water nymphs. Nymphs are said to be mischievous and curious but not harmful. They are also said to fall in love with humans from time to time.

The most famous of the water sprites, and conceivably the most alluring, are the sirens. Stories, poems and legends about the songs of the sirens sinking ships or luring unsuspecting sailors down to their deaths are known the world over. Much less familiar are the Native American water spirits known as the Mannegishi. The Mannegishi are part of the Ojibway, Cree, Algonquin and Ottawa mythology and are believed to be river spirits. They are also known by Native Americans as the "little people" who live along the riverbanks. The Mannegishi are said to be nonthreatening unless disrespected. At those times, they can be rather malicious and will tip over canoes or kayaks—even if it drowns the passengers. In Ojibwe folklore, the Mannegishi can be seen only by medicine people or children. Other stories say they will appear to anyone and may also help people who give them gifts. With descriptions of the Mannegishi ranging from spirit beings to something akin to a Bigfoot or elemental, it is difficult to determine if they are spirit-forms or physical beings.

So who or what is it that fishermen see moving above the top of the Croton dam from time to time? It is the ghost of a small boy who fell to his death while fishing or playing or something else? There doesn't seem to be anything substantial to prove that a young boy ever fell to his death or drowned at that spot, though it could be that it happened before the dam was ever built and the boy's spirit was somehow drawn to the dam. It is believed that spirits can communicate through water as well as through electricity. This has been shown by the positive results obtained by paranormal investigators using electronic equipment and devices. Possibly, the apparition is drawn to the power generated by the plant. Then again, he may not be a ghost at all. Perhaps he is a water spirit that people mistake for a child, a water sprite or one of the Mannegishi. This may be why the apparition is seen hovering above the wall and not on it. He doesn't seem to be malicious in any way.

He does seem to be forlorn or forgotten. Perhaps this is why he sobs. Many times, those with empathic abilities can communicate with spirits to help them pass over. Given the location of this small spirit, it would be almost impossible for a medium to make contact with him to find out why he sobs, so for now, the little fisher boy's tears may go on.

CHAPTER 11

TIME TO CLOCK OUT: GHOSTS OF THE BIG RED MILL (ROWE MANUFACTURING)

As you walk alongside the railroad tracks near the Muskegon River, dark, foreboding ruins become visible through the trees, jutting up from the hill like a medieval fortress. Shards of a battered and crumbling foundation lie strewn across the ground, covered in moss and overgrown with weeds. Streams of water cascade from the remnants of weather-worn troughs. The sound of surging water is deafening. In the moonlight, the dull gray cement slabs look much like gravestones, and the entire scene has a bizarre, disorienting quality surrounding it. Near the graffiti-covered cement ruins, there is a sense of gloom and sadness. Here, in this isolated spot in the town of Newaygo, is a building that time has forgotten: the Rowe Manufacturing Company. Within the rugged expanse of brushy undergrowth that was once a significant part of Newaygo's vibrant manufacturing hub lies a completely destroyed piece of the town's as well as the county's history. In its heyday, it stood four stories tall, employed over three hundred men and contributed a great deal to the town's expansion and growth. Now, this crumbling, decaying structure is rumored to be haunted. Throughout its history, hundreds of workers passed through its doors. Do they haunt it still? Some people think so.

The Rowe Manufacturing Company, founded in 1905 by Joseph Henry Rowe, is now almost totally hidden within a thick layer of trees and overgrown brush on the banks of Pennoyer Creek near two main highways. Rowe Manufacturing was an impressive factory that began as the Portland Cement Company. Before that, the Big Red Mill, one of the area's

Logging tools display. *Heritage Museum of Newaygo County. Author photo.*

first sawmills, operated on the site. It is now a mass of crumbling cement slabs jutting out of the landscape, its demise hastened by the swift waters of Pennoyer Creek coursing through it. Over a hundred years after Rowe Manufacturing began, what remains is the lowest level of the foundation, the outside wall jutting up from the surrounding landscape. Enclosures that were once rooms now open up across the hill in black, yawning rectangular pits and large cement pieces, reminiscent of tall gravestones poking curiously through the weeds. A waterfall made by the water gushing through a trough into the river is still visible. The water pours down in cascades, churning and foaming as it hits the stream below. You can sense the immense, unstoppable power of this water as it rushes through to join the creek. This unstoppable force, once used to power the factory, has now ensured it destruction. The factory's placement on Pennoyer Creek at its entrance into the Muskegon Lake was for the sole purpose of taking advantage of the power generated by the water. Pennoyer Creek was a vital asset to the fledging company, as it powered a one-hundred-horsepower turbine engine beneath the plant, generated by a waterwheel. Waterwheels with water flowing over an upright are a familiar sight. However, this wheel was different in that it was vertical. The water flowed around it in order to turn the wheel. The power generated surged through long shafts that ran throughout the building. Belts ran from

Rowe Manufacturing Company ruins. *Screen capture from YouTube video "Is This Abandoned Mill Haunted?" Darren Dykhouse, Lakeshore Paranormal, 2021. https://www.youtube.com/@ LakeshoreParanormal. Used with permission.*

the wheel to the shafts; then pulleys ran to the machinery powering it, with clutches to adjust flow and speed.

The Rowe Manufacturing Company, like many other businesses in Newaygo County, owed much of its early beginnings to the lumber era. It made a variety of wooden products used in furniture and architectural manufacturing, as well as school and factory benches. Rowe's products and accessories were in high demand, especially in the Grand Rapids area, which was a major producer of furniture. Its products became known through the distribution of its catalog worldwide. The company started out employing six workers. Later on, upward of thirty people were employed during its busiest times. Unfortunately, the new plant had been in operation for only a short time when a fire completely destroyed it, along with a house and several barns across the river. However, this didn't stop Rowe.

Ambitious and enterprising, Rowe was the embodiment of the self-made man. He was born in 1874 in Hastings, Michigan, to a family of modest means. At eighteen, he was selling ladders for a Grand Rapids company, going door to door. He then worked for Berkey & Gay Furniture Company in Grand Rapids and Furniture City Dowel Company for some time, but from an early age, he had wanted to own his own business. He eventually founded a company in Allegan along with his brother, having gained the necessary experience at his previous business. Henry Rowe came to Newaygo with the sole intent of purchasing a dowel machine. Little did he know at the time that it would become his permanent home. That same year, he founded

Rowe Manufacturing in Newaygo. After settling there, he married Della Mae Minthorn in 1913. After a fire destroyed the building, he moved the company into an old redbrick building, which he then refinished with white aluminum siding. Unfortunately, in 1967, another fire put the company permanently out of business and ended what was once a great beacon of hope and enterprise in the community. In the aftermath, the building was left to the ravages of time, a place only a ghost would find hospitable.

Are these ruins haunted? Judging by the interest paid to the site in recent years by paranormal investigators and some of their findings, some people believe so. Quite a number of people have explored these factory ruins in Newaygo in recent years, because of both their historic significance and the rumors that they are haunted. In spite of the fresh air and the invigorating sensation one feels being so near the creek, this is a place where nature is doing its best to recover from the heavy burden that the years of lumbering and manufacturing placed on it. Indeed, a heaviness of heart and sense of misery are palpable as one nears the decaying structure. There was much industry, diligence, duty and toil connected to this piece of land and probably much personal turmoil as well. It is believed that earthbound spirits need a source of energy in order to stay on the physical plane, so they will attach themselves or a place, object or person. These spirits can attach themselves to buildings as well as places, especially near or over bodies of water. If there are ghosts here, perhaps they are confused. Some speculate that spirits do not exist in our time and are aware of only their own time; if so, to them, the factory is still as they remember it. They have become bound to the place because it is familiar to them or because they do not know that they are deceased. Several investigations have picked up positive results on electronic devices near the ruins. Some were rather significant, with strange, jumbled communication coming through, from random words to snippets of sentences. While a few paranormal investigators have picked up positive evoked voice phenomenon (EVP) readings when nearing the site, it is unknown if these readings indicated the presence of an earthbound spirit or residual psychic energy. It also isn't known who, if anyone, died while working at the Rowe company or any of the previous companies on the site. Consequently, the exact nature or source of those EVP readings cannot be determined. In any place where a person or people have spent a lot of time, residual energy can remain imprinted on the environment, especially if there were strong emotions present. This lingering energy, especially if unpleasant or negative, can often leave a heavy or dense feeling, which can be sensed by empathic people.

Although the wheel of time has forgotten this place, and nature is doing its best to erase its existence, it will continue to exist as a part of Newaygo in one form or another. For over a hundred years, a succession of companies operated on or very near this site: the Big Red Mill, Portland Cement Company, a pail company and Rowe Manufacturing. These companies collectively employed hundreds of men and enabled them to earn a living. They also contributed greatly to the expansion of the county, helping to ensure that it grew and thrived. In addition, while most of their names may be forgotten, those who labored here were just as vital to the county's growth as the businesses that employed them.

The rumors that these ruins are haunted may never be proven true, but maybe they do not need to be. It may be enough that the stories remain attached to the place like a spirit attaches itself to an object, ensuring that it continues to exist. Thus, the story is what gives the Rowe factory that sense of "ghostliness." One has only to look at photographs of the building's sad demise to get a sense of desolation. However, the area is dangerous. There are sudden drop-offs, some of which go down into the creek. Thus, due to the crumbing nature of the building, as well as other hazards, it is dangerous as well as forbidden to go onto the property. It is private property and posted with "no trespassing" signs. Henry Rowe was very much beloved in Newaygo, known for his love of people as well as his sense of humor. He was active in the community, was village president for several years, was a member of the chamber of commerce and served on the village council. Rowe died at the age of ninety in 1964. Fortunately, his legacy and dream were not forgotten. Even now, he is remembered fondly as a man whose vision, fortitude, work ethic and love of the community helped make Newaygo the thriving city that it is. After a hundred years of operation, the sound of industry was silenced. The Rowe Manufacturing building, an integral part of the Newaygo's story, was shut down and the workers sent home. The entire structure was soon demolished, leaving only memories—and, if the stories are to be believed, a few ghosts. If the ghosts of some long-ago laborers still haunt the Rowe factory, perhaps they are unaware that their workday is done and that it is time to go home.

CHAPTER 12
TWIN TRAGEDY: PREMONITIONS AND A GHOSTLY VISITATION

This is a personal story related to me that occurred in a rural area of Newaygo County. The names have been changed and specific details left out for privacy considerations. This story involves hauntings, elements of telepathy between twins, precognition and spirit communication. Melissa, soon to be a senior in high school, had a near-fatal accident that would seemingly be connected to an unforeseen tragedy, one that would change her life forever. She told me that on the day of the accident, it was cold and raining, and the road became quite slick. As she came up over a hill, there was a semitruck completely blocking the road, which she couldn't avoid. The accident left her with some major injuries, including a spinal compression, fractured teeth, broken ribs and a broken knee. Melissa had an identical twin sister, Marcie, with whom she was extremely close. Melissa said they were both very artistically talented and could communicate without words. They were very much in tune with each other, so much so that if one sister felt pain, the other sister did, too.

This uncanny connection would become undeniable a few months after the accident. The last few months had been very difficult for Melissa, and she would often have nightmares about the car accident, often reliving the event over and over. One night in February, the nightmares took a more disturbing turn. This time, it was not Melissa in the car hitting the semi: it was her twin sister, Marcie. Melissa was unnerved by this. To her, it did not feel like a dream; it felt like it had really happened. As she got ready for school, she could not shake the feeling that something bad was going to happen to Marcie. The twins had been sharing their car, and Marcie had it that day. Marcie had been staying at her fiancé's house, as he had been having medical issues. As Melissa waited for Marcie to show up with the car, she became increasingly worried, because Marcie was never late. The feeling that something had happened to Marcie became overpowering. Something was wrong. She had to find her. It took some time, but she finally convinced her mother that they needed to go find Marcie. Melissa took off in search of her sister, intuitively going down the same road where she had her accident. She had gone several miles when she saw a woman standing next to a car stopped on the side of the road. The woman was vomiting. Melissa was focused on finding her sister, so she didn't think much of it. It wasn't until later that she would find out the importance of this seemingly random sight and who this woman was. In the distance, she saw a semitruck stopped across the road, completely blocking it. In order to go by it, she had to drive onto the shoulder. As she did so, she saw Marcie, lying peacefully on the grass. She had died instantly after her car was forced off the road by a drunk driver. This was the woman Melissa had seen on the side of the road. Marcie had collided with the semi, just as Melissa had seen in her nightmare.

Several months after Marcie's passing, their mother had a dream in which Marcie appeared to her. She told Melissa that the dream appeared very real to her. It was just as if Marcie was standing there in her bedroom, speaking to her in person. In the dream, she asked Marcie why she had come back. Marcie told her it was because she had forgotten something. This rather strange reply was soon to become clear. Marcie's fiancé, Lee, died later on that evening. Marcie and Lee were inseparable. Melissa often called him Marcie's Romeo. After going to the emergency room, saying he had been bitten by a rattlesnake, he was given an antitoxin but later died. Melissa and Lee were also friends, and she believes his spirit has made itself known to her on more than one occasion after he passed. She said whenever she visited his parents' home, his favorite songs would play on the radio or the boom box. She would also hear footsteps in the hallway and his bedroom when no one was there. This would happen every night for months after he died. This is a very tragic story, to be sure, yet a poignant one. It is a story of love, hope and the immutable bond that connects us all, both in life and in death. "Romeo, Romeo, wherefore art thou Romeo?" He has crossed the veil and joined his Juliet in that great theater in the hereafter.

CHAPTER 13

MY GHOSTS OF CHRISTMAS PAST: I.J. ROBINSON BLOCK BUILDING

It was opening day for Newaygo's annual Christmas Walk Shopping and Celebration. This is when the shops on State Street keep their doors open for late-night shopping every Friday and Saturday throughout the holiday season. This yearly event is a community favorite and attended by folks from miles around, and for good reason. The entire downtown is aglow with holiday cheer as the townsfolk come out to enjoy the merriment with friends and family. Christmas Walk is the kind of delightful and unique homespun event not often seen in larger cities, certain to be a memorable experience for many attending. Strolling along State Street during Christmas Walk, one may feel they have been transported back in time or are in a vintage holiday movie: lights twinkle all along the main thoroughfare, and storefronts are adorned with festive garlands and lights. Opening ceremonies start at Brooks Park, and State Street is transformed into a wonderland. A horse-drawn wagon carrying holiday passengers meanders down the street, the sound of Christmas carols wafts through the air and the inviting aroma of hot chocolate, cookies and other delights tops off the perfect holiday experience. This is a Christmas celebration in the Heart of the River.

It was my first visit to Newaygo, and I was immediately struck by its unique charm. It was a cold Friday and had been threatening rain all day but was quite mild for a typical Michigan December. Per Mother Nature's usual, our winters tend to have us breaking out the mittens, boots and snow shovels by the end of October. I had arrived early and had not yet had dinner, so I decided to find someplace to get warmed up and grab a bite

Former I.J. Robinson Block building. *Author photo.*

before the opening ceremonies. Looking around, I spotted what looked like the perfect place, a charming little coffee shop nestled cozily in an 1880s brick building once known as the I.J. Robinson Block. I went in to check out the fare. By its warm atmosphere and friendly staff, I knew I was in the right place. I sat down at the bar and ordered a cup of coffee and a dinner salad. As I waited, I looked around at the beautiful architecture and interior. Rustic brick walls, warm colors, low lighting and smoothly polished wooden floors, tables and chairs gave the place a soft, warm glow, very much in keeping with the Victorian-era building. Several minutes into my salad, I happened to glance toward the front of the building. Just as I did, I caught a glimpse of something a bit curious—nothing menacing, just out of the ordinary. It was a thin, almost transparent wispy haze moving across the room, going from the corner toward the front windows. As I continued to watch, it disappeared either in front of or through the door; I wasn't sure. I was taken aback by this and tried to figure out what I had seen. Later that evening, after the festivities had ended, I stopped in again to visit with a friend who lives in the area. We chatted for a while, again sitting at the bar. Several times during our visit, I felt a fleeting cold sensation near the empty stool to the right of me, where I had set my purse. The temperature drop was very noticeable. Noticing that the building appeared quite old, I wondered if perhaps there was a bit of residual spirit energy left in the building. These incidents did make an impression on me, but at no point did I feel threatened by them. In fact, while I found them curious, they did not detract from my being very impressed by the building's historic beauty and the comfortable, warm atmosphere within.

However, later on, as I retired for the night to my hotel room, I was still thinking about the strange mist and cold sensation I had experienced; thus, they may have been a factor in the strange dream I had that night. In the dream, I saw the Robinson building decked out in holiday finery and people were milling about me, looking in store windows, walking along or conversing with one another—though instead of it being the modern day, they appeared to be dressed in clothing from a prior era, possibly from Victorian times. Next, I saw myself lying on the bed, asleep, as a spirit, pale and shapeless, came through the door and hovered silently above the bed, looking down at me as I slept. After this, it seemed as though the spirit became me, looking down at myself. Needless to say, when I awoke, I spent some time considering the high strangeness of this dream. Given that I have always been quite enamored of the Victorian era, as well as Charles Dickens's stories, I could not help noting the seeming similarity between

Dickens's most famous ghost story, *A Christmas Carol*, and my dream. It is quite possible that my fondness for Dickens's story contributed to my dream. Truly, given its features, the Robinson Block at Christmastime would have fit quite marvelously into one of Dickens's tales.

This Victorian-era building, originally owned by I.J. Robinson, was built after the fire of 1883 destroyed virtually all the downtown buildings, with the exception of two. Robinson himself suffered property losses of $300 in the fire. The building changed hands over the years, being purchased by George Day at one time. In 1903, Day sold it to Art Dysinger, who opened an art gallery. After that, it was purchased by Russell Shepard, a Newaygo attorney. In those early years, the downtown area had thriving businesses of varying types: Joe Butler's Hotel, which was next to Robinson's; the Surplice building, which was later the State Hotel; and Reinhardt's Vaudette, which was located in the Surplice building. Edward's Hardware later became Walker's Bait Shop, and the Macabee building held Soper's Drug Store. Some of these businesses were impacted by several fires, one of which caused an immense amount of damage.

Newaygo's first big fire was at the Newaygo Company's sawmill some time before 1870. The second one was in 1874 and started at Luton Sinclair's drugstore. It was a total loss, and damage was also done to buildings nearby. The fire also spread to Soper's drugstore. However, the biggest and most memorable fire happened in 1883, which almost completely destroyed downtown Newaygo. By the time the fire was contained, it had completely destroyed thirty buildings and caused $50,000 in property losses. It seemed almost inevitable that another fire would happen. It was well known that the buildings along State Street were a virtual firetrap, as they were all constructed of wood. Unfortunately, fire safety measures seemed to take a backseat to implementing changes. For example, even the fire pump and hose system located in the public square were not usable. This situation was not overlooked as a concern by townsfolk. Regrettably, their fears were realized that fateful morning in 1883 when another fire ravaged the town. There were varying stories about the origin of the fire. The fire alarm had sounded a little after eight o'clock that Sunday morning when flames tore through the roof of a building owned by E.L. Gray, which housed a jewelry and news store and also had apartments on the upper level.

The fire spread out westward to Edward's hardware store and eastward to the home of J.H. Standish, but it didn't stop there. Across the street, it devastated Brooks House, the pride and staple of Newaygo. It then took out a meat market, and a law and printing business, as well as many other

Victorian-style clock on a corner in front of the Newaygo County Museum and Heritage Center of Newaygo County. *Author photo.*

buildings. When it got to Raider's brick building, the flames were hampered somewhat. Dispatches were sent out to Grand Rapids and Woodville for help, and engines from each place soon arrived, along with men who set to work attempting to contain the fire. After it became clear that the fire could not be contained, the community quickly rallied together, removing as much property and goods as they could. After a day and a night, the fire was brought under control but not before it had ravaged the village. When morning arrived, the scene was one of utter desolation. Many had lost everything, and over one hundred people were left homeless. Even so, the pioneering spirit prevailed. Townspeople quickly took to helping out their neighbors, salvaging essential goods and property. They began making plans for rebuilding. It wasn't long before the rebuilding began. In fact, before the winter winds blew, the Courtright building had sprung up where Brooks House had long stood. After the fire, regulations were enacted and better fire safety measures implemented. In addition, from that time onward, all new buildings along that corridor would use brick architecture. It was good choice, not only for preventing another devastating fire but also for giving the downtown area a uniquely delightful Victorian flare. This popular and well-recognized style remains apparent in many of the buildings constructed after the fire.

It is easy to see why styles from the Victorian era continue to be immensely popular, in architecture as well as in other facets of society. They hark back to a time of grace and simplicity as well as wholesomeness. The use of brick and masonry in construction not only resulted in the preservation of the I.J. Robinson Block and other buildings, but it also added to their charm and beauty. Stonemasonry has been used in building construction in the United States throughout its history, with many types of stone being used, from sandstone to fieldstone. Before the late 1800s, bricks were made by using molds, which made their quality somewhat unreliable. However, after 1870, an extrusion process made them more durable. Bricks are held together by the use of mortar. Early mortar was made of lime, additives and sand and tended to be rather soft. When Portland cement came into use as an additive, this made mortar more rigid, adding to its strength. Although masonry is one of the most durable building components, it is subject to damage if not maintained properly or if abrasive materials are used during cleaning. By the nineteenth century, bricks were being manufactured. These machine-made bricks were stronger and more uniform and could be made in a variety of colors, enabling builders to create decorative patterning on outside walls. In addition, because the manufactured bricks were of uniform size with sharper edges, bricklaying was made easier. One drawback was their increased cost. For this reason, many times, they were only used on façades. For a time, in the 1960s and 1970s, the downtown area was blighted by many dilapidated and empty buildings; however, over the last ten years, the City of Newaygo has implemented improvements and renovations that helped the downtown business district grow and thrive. Many storefronts were given new façades, parking issues were eased and other improvements were made, creating an attractive and inviting business area that's become a vibrant focal point for merchants and entrepreneurs. Newaygo's downtown is now the Newaygo Community's Principal Shopping District, with a variety of uses, including residential, recreational, cultural, retail and entertainment. The downtown's

Northwoods Building, downtown Newaygo. *Author photo.*

Downtown Newaygo, present day. *Author photo.*

Left: Old State Theater building, which now houses mixed-use shops and a bed-and-breakfast. *Author photo.*

Below: A serene spot to rest on State Street. *Author photo.*

renewed vigor as a vibrant hub of activity envelops within it a sense of warmth and cohesiveness that's often missing in large cities. Truly, the Heart of the River embraces all who enter, from near and far.

I do not know what it was I saw and felt that December evening. Very possibly, it was a trick of the eyes, as I was hungry and tired from the trip, or the expectation of experiencing something paranormal, given that old buildings sometimes hold spirits. However, there have been others who believed they experienced "spooky" things within the walls of the Robinson building; indeed, there are said to be many such tales. Imaginably, these tales involve something similar to what I experienced. Perhaps they involve shadows, cold drafts, footsteps or other strange things that are typical of paranormal displays or residual spirit energy. In the hundred-plus years this building has stood, many people have passed within its walls, and many businesses have operated within. If there was a spirit present that day, maybe the building is holding onto some residual energy from those long-ago Victorian days. Given the time of year and the festive atmosphere that enveloped the town in mystical, wondrous enchantment that evening, perhaps what I experienced was from a Christmas held there long ago—maybe even the Ghost of Christmas Past.

CHAPTER 14

FLYING BEAR BOOKS & CREPERIE: COMMUNITY GHOST STORIES

For book lovers, there is nothing better than a cozy bookstore, one where you can browse to your heart's content until the perfect book makes itself known to you. Flying Bear Books & Creperie (Flying Bear Books for short) located at 79 State Road in Newaygo, Michigan, is just that sort of cozy spot. This is a place where one can savor their love of books, destress from the workday and connect with friends. Flying Bear Books is owned and operated by Eric and Krystal Johnson—lifelong residents of Newaygo, having grown up in the downtown area. After working in a variety of disciplines in the business world, from business analysis to project management, they decided they wanted a change of pace. So when the bookstore became available, it seemed the perfect choice. They bought it in September 2022, and it has been growing ever since. Shortly after the bookstore opened, they added a creperie, bringing the delightful addition of crepes and coffee to this already charming place. Crepes, coffee and books all in one place? Sounds like a book lover's paradise. Along with its large selection of books, Flying Bear Books has become a popular local gathering place for creativity, art, comedy and music holding open mic nights, as well as book signings, musical performances, comedy shows and various other creative events and shows.

The unique charm of Flying Bear Books is evident as soon as you walk through the door. It is reminiscent of the feeling one gets sitting by a roaring fire on a cold winter's night, reading a mystery, a ghost story or whatever your favorite genre is. It has the best of both worlds: a snug coffee shop and creperie where the aroma of coffee and crepes blends in with the comforting

Flying Bear Books & Creperie, a popular community hub for events as well as books. *Author photo.*

smell of books. It's like coming home: the ideal place to spend some peaceful moments. Yet if you feel like being entertained, you can find that there, too. In addition to hosting author and other unique events, the Johnsons are very much invested in bringing the artistic, creative and musical worlds to the fore, holding music events, hosting exhibits and showing the work of local artists. Of course, there are plenty of unique books to be found at Flying Bear Books, too, with its large stock of both fiction and nonfiction titles for the entire family. Their children's section includes over six thousand books.

Reading ghost stories can be thrilling and fun, especially the kind that give you goosebumps or make you wonder. One thing that could possibly be better than reading a ghost story is getting together as a group and sharing ghost stories. If it happens in a bookstore where some actual ghost hunting was done, even better. While it's unclear if Flying Bear Books is haunted, some interesting EVP activity was picked up on a ghost hunt performed back in 2022. The Newaygo community was invited to attend a ghost story forum held at Flying Bear Books in 2023, which garnered a lot of interest. Many came to share their favorite local ghost stories and legends as well as offer interesting bits of local history. Some of the stories were well known in the area; some were previously unknown.

The Breather

The Breather story, a story within a story, related by Flying Bear Books & Creperie owner Eric Johnson, has probably been told around many a campfire on a crisp autumn night. It has no doubt scared the living daylights out of a few campers. It begins with a camper who was murdered by having his throat cut, and now his ghost appears to campers as a warning. The first thing they will notice is the sound of raspy breathing outside their tent or cabin, said to be the sound of the ghost's breathing through the gaping hole in his neck. It's uncertain where or how this story got started, but it is definitely one that could make you zip that tent flap up tight before you go to sleep—if you can sleep.

The story is one that Eric Johnson heard as a child while growing up in the town of Newaygo. Although the story was told among the differing groups of people with whom he socialized, the details were always the same. Eric recollected that the first time he heard the story, he was a preteen and was camping with some friends along the "Mighty" Muskegon River. Camping was pretty much the thing that preteens who lived in this rural area along the edge of the Manistee Forest did. As the group sat around the campfire, talk soon centered on the story of the Breather. Some had heard it before; a few had not. Some said that the story started with a group of kids who were camping next to the Muskegon River, but no one really knew exactly who started the story or when. None of that mattered, because with the night chill in the air and the fire roaring, it was the perfect night for it. The Breather is told like a never-ending tale that comes with a warning, a test and a challenge. As the story progresses, each telling of the story around a campfire leads to *that* camper being murdered, and so on and so on. The challenging part of the story is that if you hear the ghost breathing, you are to yell "Breather!" three times, and hopefully that will save you from the Breather.

Eric related that the story begins with a group of kids who were camping near the Muskegon River. The sun was setting. They knew it would be dark soon, so they were gathering sticks to build a fire. Someone in the group pointed out the silhouette of a person standing on the other side of the river. The weird silhouette seemed to be staring at them rather eerily. Later, as they sat around the fire, they challenged one another to tell a scary story. Someone in the group commented that the creepy silhouette reminded them of the Breather story. One of them replied, "Well, they say it happened right here in these woods. This is where he got his throat sliced, and now he goes around slicing campers' throats that see him." Even though no one believed the story, they all still wanted to hear it. After they had finished taking turns telling stories, things got quiet, and they decided to go to sleep. They snuggled up in their sleeping bags in the large domed tent and made small talk until they drifted off to sleep. Eric says,

We all have those times when we are awake but immersed in a state that slowly realizes: this is real. Well, in that state, the entire group was each awake but unaware of all the others awake as well, as they were listening to something or someone outside their tent breathing. It wasn't a panting or out-of-breath breathing but a slow and deliberate in-and-out deep inhale—as you just tried yourself reading this.

As their eyes adjusted to things and they began to pinpoint the direction of this uncanny deep, deep breathing, they realized it was just outside the side wall of the tent. It was autumn, and the air was chilly. The rising full moon illuminated that side of the tent and cast shadows of the trees as well as a strange silhouette. The silhouette did not seem to belong. They could see puffs of air swirling around it, creating a dense fog in the moonlight—coming from its throat and not its mouth. It was at this point that the group became fully awake, and they focused all their attention on the man standing outside their tent.

The group then started to chant, "One, two, three... Breather, breather, breather," like in the other legends they had heard about. The succeeding story then makes another round, with a new group of campers listening to the story in a continuing cycle.

Eric ends the story with its challenge and warning, saying,

When you are camping along the Muskegon River and the sun is going down, look to the other side of the river and see if you can see Breather, with his puffs of smoke billowing out of his throat. Then remember, if you do see him, you may be woken up by the deep and heavy breathing through his throat. Then it's on you to scream... BREATHER BREATHER BREATHER!

Auntie's Spooky Doll and the Haunted Closet

The following story from the town of Newaygo was shared by Jan Smith. It involves her and her family and is rather terrifying, especially if you are one of those who find dolls creepy—even ones that aren't haunted. This happened at a house where Jan, her husband and their children once lived. While there were a lot of really strange things going on at the time, some of most bizarre and frightening of these seemed to center on a closet in a bathroom and an antique doll in a bedroom. Jan's daughter was very frightened of sleeping in the room, and the reasons why soon became frightfully clear. Jan said that the bathroom door would be tied shut, but when her daughter woke up in the night, the string would be lying on the floor and the door would be open. Her daughter would use the bathroom downstairs during the night. When she returned to her bed, the doll that had been on the floor would be sitting up on the end of her bed. At night, after she went to bed, she would see toys and articles being thrown out of the closet by an unseen hand. Toys and articles that were put away in the closet the night before would be strewn across the floor in the morning. The doll had belonged to an aunt who had passed away. Once, after the room had been cleaned, the doll was set on the floor. Later on, it was found on the bed, even though no one else had been in the room. Jan's young daughter became so frightened of the doll that she drew black crosses all over the doll's face—much to the dismay of her mother, since this doll was very old and a treasured family heirloom. It is unknown whether the strange events stopped after this—hopefully so.

Children have been playing with dolls for many hundreds of years, but oddly enough, they often give people the creeps. There isn't a lot of research out there to explain exactly why some people are afraid of dolls, but one theory proposed by Masahiro Mori in 1970 suggests fear is a normal human response when confronted with something that is almost humanlike, as would be in the case when interacting with a robot. Thus, when we see a humanlike robot act in a manner that is not consistent with human behavior—for example, eye movements that do not line up with other facial expressions—we may tend to get creeped out by it. Mori called this feeling the "uncanny valley." Dolls seem to have that same effect on some people. Obviously, not everyone is afraid of dolls, although fear of dolls has been greatly enhanced by popular culture in recent years. Perhaps this fear is also because of the way that dolls seem to stare at us through eyes that are not real and do not see. Further adding to the uncanny valley feeling is that although they look lifelike, they do not display emotions, which is one thing that makes us human. If you wish to go deep into the uncanny valley or right down into the paranormal, just imagine that they are basically empty shells inside, ripe for something supernatural to take over.

OTHER FASCINATING STORIES TOLD during the forum included accounts of strange nightmares about a ghostly dog and a shapeshifting entity. The story of a family having nightmares about a large dog jumping through the window if the shade was not pulled down was quite inexplicable, especially as they were also plagued by other paranormal phenomena. A local legend involving what was described as a shapeshifting entity or spirit was also quite intriguing. Local legend has it that this apparition or shape-shifting entity is seen along area trails from time to time. This was shared by a local historian and artist. It was a very curious tale indeed, full of wonder and mystery as well as beauty. There are a lot of different components interwoven into it, including mythology, Native American folklore, the paranormal and perhaps even UFOlogy. Historically, shapeshifting beings are very reminiscent of the owl manitou from Native American mythology. Owls as shape-shifting spirit animals are a well-known theme in Native American folklore. Additionally, sightings of owls also feature prominently in UFOlogy, during which a person thinks they are seeing an owl but is in fact seeing an alien entity. In UFOlogy, this is known as a "cover" and believed to be part of the alien abduction phenomenon. Theoretically, the person will believe they are seeing an owl because the alien has put this cover identity into the person's mind.

The stories shared that day at Flying Bear Books & Creperie showed that many have a keen interest in ghosts, hauntings and other mysteries in and around Newaygo County. This discussion was all done in a light manner and with a willingness to explore these experiences, legends and stories, making for a very enjoyable event. Just as one would huddle around a campfire, bundled up to the chin in a blanket, roasting marshmallows on a brisk Michigan night, the coming together of the community to share and listen to some of Newaygo County's ghost stories brought excited anticipation as well as an atmosphere of community. After all, these are Newaygo County's ghosts and legends, and they are an integral part of the community.

EPILOGUE

Newaygo County's official history dates to around the same time as the history of Michigan itself. Undoubtedly, this has given rise to thousands of stories chronicling the building of its settlements and towns, as well as to stories of the pioneering men and women who helped them grow and thrive. Conversely, there are other stories, too, perhaps not so well known, of spirits, ghosts, hauntings and mysterious places. Nevertheless, the true spirit of Newaygo County is in its resilience and cohesiveness as a community. This resilience has seen the county through much turbulent change over the years, and it continues to weather the storms and be all the stronger for it. That same pioneering spirit that drove the people of Newaygo County to create cities and towns out of the wilderness, as well as endure the collapse of the lumber and manufacturing industries, will enable them to continue to thrive, no matter what comes. Thus, if Newaygo County has a few ghosts wandering about, more than likely folks here would take it all in stride. Besides, for the most part, these ghosts don't seem to be of the troublesome sort. They have effectively blended into the folklore and mythology of the area, giving it just enough mystery to make things thrilling but not enough to frighten anyone away. Though, to be sure, people in Newaygo County don't scare easily. Some may actually like the idea that their house was haunted; the more the merrier, right? In fact, the people of Newaygo County, with their community spirit and good nature, would undoubtedly find a way to make a ghost feel at home.

Ghosts are often to be found haunting houses or buildings but can haunt public spaces, too, including roads, forests, lakes or parks. Even those ghost stories intrigue us. Folklorists believe this is because anyone can visit these areas, so it makes the stories about them feel more personal. People can become part of the story or can engage with it in some way. This may be why some ghost stories become the stuff of legends. They get passed down from one generation to another and from one place to another. Throughout history, the population circulates tales of ghosts known to be in specific places. Some ghost stories may even act as moral lessons or warnings, especially to the young. Stories that echo cultural beliefs have the ability to disseminate widely or become ingrained in community lore, thus becoming legends.

People who love to read understand the shivery coziness one feels when reading a ghost story. Ghost stories or paranormal unknowns may make us fearful. Fortunately, sharing and listening to ghost stories actually makes us feel closer, although this solace and sense of safety may last only until the story is over. Most cultures around the world have ghost stories. They are journeys into the unknown, where in our imaginations lie the specters or monsters. When we are telling or listening to ghost stories, we are not alone; as a result, they may help us overcome those imaginary fears. Being with others who may have the same fears may give us a sense of control. Lastly, ghost stories, like other stories, take us to other places or other times, allowing us to escape the mundane world for a time. We get a sense of closeness to others when sharing or hearing them, to be sure. Certainly, it is that same underlying sense of community that weaves its way through Newaygo County, connecting all that has kept these ghost stories alive.

We often tend to think of history in terms of reading about it, seeing old photographs or visiting a museum. However, when you walk into a building that has stood the test of time for over one hundred years, you can also feel it. The energies of all that went on within its walls feel present. Listening to the stories passed on from generation to generation also makes history seem more alive. Many of these ghost stories and legends have been passed down for years. We may never know if any of them are true. But if they can tell us anything, it is that perhaps what some call ghosts or spirits are in fact simply the residual energy of all those who lived out their lives in those spaces, thus leaving a spiritual imprint on the environment, which can be felt and sensed or sometimes seen. It remains like a psychic history or biography of sorts, often because many generations have come and gone within those same spaces, overlapping over time. It is often said that history is written by the winners and that ordinary people do not often make the history books. If these places do indeed hold the imprinted psychic energies of people who lived or spent time there, then they might take heart to know that they were not lost to time. While their names may never appear in a history book and their portraits many never hang in a museum, the very environment has written their story within its essence, a psychic book waiting to be read. While skeptics tend to regard the paranormal as fiction, hoax or misidentification, there is much evidence to the contrary. In addition to multiple credible witness accounts spanning many years, much data has been gathered by electronic means. This gives the shadowy realm of the paranormal, with its ghosts, spirits, entities and high strangeness, a level of credibility that was previously not available. Truly, we may one day discover what lies beyond the veil that separates the living from the dead. For this reason, we should keep an open mind about the paranormal, as all may not be as it seems. We may find that ghosts indeed walk the earth, maybe even in Newaygo County. These stories may give us a peek into what lies beyond. At the very least, they open up the possibility, with the foremost question in mind: Are they true? This is for the reader to decide.

BIBLIOGRAPHY

Andrews, Nadine. Personal communication. Live research/ghost story forum. Flying Bear Books & Creperie, Newaygo, MI. June 7, 2023. Interviewed by Marie Cisneros. Story appears in chapter 2, "Good Night, Ladies."

Anonymous (various). Personal communications. Live research/ghost story forum. Flying Bear Books & Creperie, Newaygo, MI. June 7, 2023. Interviewed by Marie Cisneros. Stories appear in chapter 1, "Days of Decadence"; chapter 7, "A Pioneering Spirit"; and chapter 14, "Flying Bear Books & Creperie."

Anonymous. Personal communication. April 12, 2023. Facebook messenger. Interviewed by Marie Cisneros. Story appears in chapter 12, "Twin Tragedy."

Anonymous. Personal communication. May 2, 2023. Telephone. Interviewed by Marie Cisneros. Story appears in chapter 14, "Flying Bear Books & Creperie."

Anonymous. Personal conversation. March 25, 2023. Telephone. Interviewed by Marie Cisneros. Story appears in chapter 9, "The Night Shift."

Barritt, Amy. "Forgotten Stories: Michigan's Lumber Pikes." *Grand Traverse Journal* (blog), July 1, 2017. Accessed April 17, 2023. https://gtjournal.tadl.org/2017/michigans-lumber-pikes.

Beliefnet. "What Are Orbs?" https://www.beliefnet.com.

Bernard, Sandi. Personal communication. Live research/ghost story forum. Flying Bear Books & Creperie, Newaygo, MI. June 7, 2023. Interviewed by Marie Cisneros. Story appears in chapter 2, "Good Night, Ladies."

Blind Squirrel Tavern. http://www.blindsquirreltavern.com.

Britannica. "Al Capone." https://www.britannica.com/biography/Al-Capone.

Burton, Neel. "The Symbolism of Snakes." *Psychology Today*, May 11, 2021. https://www.psychologytoday.com.

Carpenter, Jen (host). "Swamp Monster." *Violent Ends: A True Crime Podcast*. Episode 49, March 24, 2020. Produced by Ben Goldman. https://www.sodeadpodcast.com/podcasts/ep49.

Cisneros, Marie Helena. *Haunted Muskegon*. Charleston, SC: The History Press, 2022.

City of Grant, Michigan. "Grant Farmer's Market." Accessed July 25, 2023. https://www.cityofgrantmi.com/farmersmarket.html.

———. "Water Tower Park." Accessed July 25, 2023. https://cityofgrantmi.com/cityparks.html.

———. "Welcome!" Accessed July 19, 2023. http://www.cityofgrantmi.com.

City of Newaygo. "Welcome Information." https://www.newaygo.gov.

City of White Cloud, Michigan. https://www.cityofwhitecloud.org.

Cryptid. "Is Bigfoot a Forest Spirit?" Exemplore, August 6, 2022. https://exemplore.com/cryptids/Bigfoot-Forest-Spirit.

Dary, David. *Frontier Medicine: From the Atlantic to the Pacific, 1492–1941*. Published. New York, NY: Borzoi Books, 2008.

Dickens, Charles. *A Christmas Carol*. London, England: Chapman & Hall, 1843.

Dogwood Center for the Performing Arts. https://dogwoodcenter.com.

Downtown Threadz. https://downtownthreadz.com.

Dykhouse, Darren. "Is This Mill Haunted?" Lakeshore Paranormal. YouTube video, 26:20, January 29, 2021. https://youtu.be/An9lylVV1nM.

Emerick, Carolyn. "Nature Spirits: Elves and Fairies of the Forest." Exemplore, updated August 3, 2022. https://exemplore.com.

eReference Desk. *"First Early Inhabitants of Michigan."* Early Michigan History. https://www.ereferencedesk.com/resources/state-early-history/michigan.html.

Erickson, Monica, and Jan Cortez. "John F. Wood Sr." Newaygo County MiGenWeb. Michigan Genealogy on the Web. Part of the USGenWeb Project. https://migenweb.org/newaygo.

Evens, Suzanne. "Prohibition, Speakeasies and Finger Foods." History.com, updated August 29, 2018. https://www.history.com.

Facebook. "Life in Fremont, Michigan." Facebook Group. Accessed March 29, 2023. https://www.facebook.com.

Ferrell, David. "Beneath the Hospital, a Bewildering Labyrinth." *Los Angeles Times*, June 28, 2001. https://www.latimes.com/archives/la-xpm-2001-jun-28-me-16012-story.html

FestivalNet. "Harvest Moon Festival." Website. https://festivalnet.com.

Folklore Thursday. "Forest Folklore: Wild Gods, World Trees and Werewolves." August 5, 2021. https://folklorethursday.com.

Fountain View Assisted Living. https://fountainviewgrant.org.

Frankson, Robert. "11 Owls in Michigan [With Sounds & Pictures]. Wildyards. Updated June 13, 2013. https://wildyards.com/owls-in-michigan.

Geller, Prof. "What Is the Black Dog?" Mythology.net, updated April 8, 2017. https://mythology.net/mythical-creatures/black-dog.

Genealogy Trails. "City of Fremont." Newaygo Co, MI Genealogy and History. https://genealogytrails.com/mich/newaygo/cityfremont.html.

———. "Hotels and Resorts, Newaygo County, Michigan." https://genealogytrails.com/mich/newaygo/hotel.html.

Gerber Foundation. https://www.gerberfoundation.org.

Gianoulis, Tina. "Goth Culture." Encylopedia.com, 2019. https://www.encyclopedia.com.

Glatz, Kyle. "Poisonous Snakes in Michigan: The Snakes You Must Avoid." *A-Z Animals* (blog). November 4, 2022. https://a-z-animals.com.

Goldwasser, Max. "Fact or Fiction: Al Capone's Connection to Newaygo County." Fox 17 West Michigan, August 22, 2022. https://www.fox17online.com.

Groth, Leah. "Your Fear of Dolls Is Totally Normal, According to a Psychologist." Prevention, October 12, 2018. https://www.prevention.com.

Guardian. "Victorian Buildings: A Spotter's Guide." September 11, 2011. https://www.theguardian.com.

Habib, Raeesah. "The 11 Owl Types of Michigan and Where to Find Them." Avibirds.com. June 26, 2021. https://avibirds.com/owls-of-michigan.

Hank. "Meady & the Murders." *Hank's Lore* (blog), September 29, 2020. https://www.hankslore.com/post/meady-the-murders.

Haunted Places in Michigan (blog). Wednesday, May 10, 2006. https://ahauntinginmichigan.blogspot.com.

Heisman, Rebecca. "Know Your Nocturnal Neighbors: Nine Owl Calls to Listen For." American Bird Conservancy, September 30, 2021. https://abcbirds.org/blog21/owl-sounds.

Helgemo, Jim. "Superb Fishing in Newaygo County." Newaygo County Exploring! https://newaygocountyexploring.com.

Henderson, Alice Palmer. "Secret Ojibwa Medicine Society." The Wanderling, 1996. https://the-wanderling.com/midewiwin.html.

Hirst, Kris K. "Leshy, Slavic Spirit of the Forest." ThoughtCo, updated October 28, 2019. https://www.thoughtco.com/leshy-4774301.

Historical Marker Database. "Grant Water Tower." https://www.hmdb.org/m.asp?m=182744.

History.com Editors. "Prohibition." History.com. Updated August 12, 2022. https://www.history.com.

———. "The Roaring Twenties." Updated August 12, 2022. https://www.history.com.

Hohenadel, Kristen. "What Is Italianate Architecture?" The Spruce, updated February 19, 2023. https://www.thespruce.com.

Hoxie, Frederick E. *Encyclopedia of North American Indians: Native American History, Culture, and Life from Paleo-Indians to the Present.* New York, NY: Houghton Mifflin, 1996.

Interesting Literature (blog). "The Curious Symbolism of Snakes in Literature and Myth." https://interestingliterature.com.

Johnson, Ben. "The Great British Pub." Historic UK. https://www.historic-uk.com.

Johnson, Eric D. Personal communication. Live research/ghost story forum. Flying Bear Books & Creperie, Newaygo, MI. June 7, 2023. Interviewed by Marie Cisneros. Story appears in chapter 14, "Flying Bear Books & Creperie."

Kennedy, William. "The Myth of the Leshy Explained." Grunge, December 13, 2021. https://www.grunge.com.

"Long Lake Camp." *Newaygo County History* (October/November/December 2017): 3. Originally published in the *Newaygo Republican*, December 9, 1885. https://www.newaygocountyhistory.org/_files/ugd/6a7c7e_f05eff6859bd4cfe8547d4d099595038.pdf.

Lucchesi, Emilie Le Beau. "Why We Share Stories of Local Ghosts." *Discover*, October 20, 2021. https://www.discovermagazine.com.

Michigan Forests. "Native American Tribes in Michigan." 2017. http://www.michiganforests.com.

Michigan Haunted Houses. "La Belle de la Riviere Bed-and-Breakfast." https://www.michiganhauntedhouses.com.

MichiganLakes.com. "Croton Dam Pond." https://michiganlakes.com.

Michigan Natural Features Inventory. "Eastern Massasauga Rattlesnake." Michigan State University. https://mnfi.anr.msu.edu.

MichiganRailroads.com. "Station: White Cloud, Michigan." https://michiganrailroads.com.

Michigan State Facts & Information. "Newaygo County, Michigan History, Records, Facts and Genealogy." http://www.mymichigangenealogy.com/mi-county-newaygo.html.

Mulka, Angela. "On the Trail of Bigfoot in Northern Michigan Forests." *Midland Daily News*, October 28, 2022. https://www.ourmidland.com.

Murphy, Shea. "'Into the Woods': An Examination of Fairy Tale Forests." University of Notre Dame College of Arts and Letters. https://freshwriting.nd.edu/essays/into-the-woods-an-examination-of-fairy-tale-forests.

Muskegon Lake Watershed Partnership "Muskegon Lake." Last edited October 7, 2022. https://muskegonlake.org/muskegon-lake/

Native American Languages of the Americas "Native American Legends: Memegwesi (Mannegishi)." http://www.native-languages.org/memegwesi.htm.

Nature Blog | Project Noah. "Snakes in Mythology, Religion and Folklore." https://blog.projectnoah.org.

Near North Now. "Joy and Cheer: Newaygo Christmas Walk." December 5, 2021. https://www.nearnorthnow.com.

Nelson, Luanne Murray, interviewer. "Ron Murray-Rowe Manufacturing Disassembly" (oral history). Heritage Museum of Newaygo County, April 24, 2014. Originally posted on the Restless Viking. https://www.restless-viking.com/wp-content/uploads/2020/02/OralHistory.pdf.

Nelson's Farm Market. http://nelsonsfarmmarket.com.

Newaygo County Agricultural Fair Association "Newaygo County Fair." August 5–12, 2023. https://newaygocountyfair.org.

Newaygo County Exploring! "Croton Pond." Accessed July 27, 2023. https://newaygocountyexploring.com/project/croton-pond.

———. "Events." https://newaygocountyexploring.com/events.

———. "Ice Fishing, February." https://newaygocountyexploring.com/events.

———. "Power Paddle, June." Accessed July 31, 2023. https://newaygocountyexploring.com/events.

Newaygo County History (January/February/March 2018). https://www.newaygocountyhistory.org/_files/ugd/6a7c7e_04c8c59a3f794a0782a41760e60199ad.pdf.

Newaygo County Pioneers. "Solomon K. Riblet." Newaygo County MiGenWeb. Michigan Genealogy on the Web. Part of the USGenWeb Project. Updated October 8, 2022. https://migenweb.org/newaygo.

Newaygo Public Schools. "Lions Newaygo High School." https://www.newaygo.net.

Newaygo Republican. "Henry Rowe Obituary." November 19, 1964. https://www.restless-viking.com/wp-content/uploads/2020/02/NewsExcept.pdf.

———. "Newaygo Says Goodbye to Rowe Manufacturing Co." N.d. Heritage Museum of Newaygo County. Originally posted on the Restless Viking. https://www.restless-viking.com/wp-content/uploads/2020/02/NewsExcept.pdf.

NPI No. "Grant Medical Center in Grant." https://npino.com/primary-clinic/1437272689-grant-medical-center.

Old House Web. "Historic Exteriors: Brick and Masonry." https://www.oldhouseweb.com.

Otherworldly Oracle. "Elementals: What Is an Elemental? And the Guardians of the Watchtowers." December 1, 2020. Accessed April 17, 2023. https://otherworldlyoracle.com.

Petoskey Provisions, Gifts, & Wisdom. "These 10 Creepy Legends and Mysteries from Michigan Will Give You Goosebumps!" October 14, 2016. https://grandpashorters.com.

Portrait and Biographical Album of Newaygo County, Mich. […]. Chicago: Chapman Brothers, 1884. Available on the Internet Archive. https://archive.org/details/portraitbiograph00unse_7.

Pure Michigan. "Croton Trip Ideas." https://www.michigan.org.

———. "Fremont." https://www.michigan.org/city/fremont.

———. "Stephen F. Wessling Observatory." https://www.michigan.org.

Restless Viking. "Abandoned Powerhouses." February 12, 2020. https://www.restless-viking.com.

Rice, Jacob "Jake." "7 Types of Water Spirits." Ghosts & Monsters: A Paranormal Field Guide. February 2, 2014. https://ghostsandmonsters.com.

River Country Chamber of Commerce, Newaygo County. "Christmas Walk Newaygo 2023." https://www.rivercountrychamber.com.

Robinson, John. "Abandoned Michigan: Rowe Mfg. Factory, Newaygo." 99.1 WFMK. January 23, 2020. https://99wfmk.com/abandoned-rowe.

———. "The Boy Who Haunts the Croton Dam." 99.1 WFMK, April 14, 2020. https://99wfmk.com/croton-dam-2020.

———. "Haunted Michigan: Newaygo High School's "'Girl in Black.'" 99.1 WFMK, October 9, 2019. https://99wfmk.com/newaygo-girl-in-black.

———. "The Twisted Tale of Ghosts and Insanity at Dudgeon Swamp: Manistee National Forest." 99.1 WMFK, February 16, 2018. https://99wfmk.com/dudgeonswamp2018.

Ruby, Ilie. "Why We Love Ghost Stories." CNN, October 26, 2010. https://edition.cnn.com/2010/LIVING/10/26/we.love.ghost.stories.

Schillman, Gabe. "A Truly Magical Place." Newaygo County Exploring! April 24, 2019. https://newaygocountyexploring.com.

Seim, Jerry. "Marilyn Herringa, 70, Restored Fremont's Hauntingly Cozy Indigo Inn Herself." MLive.com, October 5, 2008. https://www.mlive.com.

Smith, Jan. Personal communication. Live research/ghost story forum. June 7, 2023. Interviewed by Marie Cisneros. Story appears in chapter 14, "Flying Bear Books & Creperie."

Sonnenberg, Mike. "Newaygo's Factory Ruins." Lost in Michigan, December 14, 2020. https://lostinmichigan.net/newaygos-factory-ruins.

Soul Java Spirit Café. "Whiskey Wood Hill." Updated July 26, 2003. https://julieeastin0.tripod.com/souljava/id10.html.

Sportsmans Bar. https://www.sportsmansnewaygo.com.

Starobinski, Jean. *A History of Medicine.* New York, NY: Hawthorn Books, 1964.

Sutherland, A. "Forest in Ancient Beliefs: Powerful Realm of Good and Evil, Ghosts, Gods and Monsters." Ancient Pages, May 19, 2016. https://www.ancientpages.com.

Taylor, Dale. *The Writer's Guide to Everyday Life in Colonial America from 1607–1783.* Cincinnati, OH: F&W Publications, 1997.

Tedsen, Kathleen, and Beverlee Rydel. *The Indigo Inn and Down Under Lounge and Grille.* Haunted Travels of Michigan. A book and web interactive experience. Holt, MI: Thunder Baby Press, July 1, 2008.

Tomes, Luke. "How Al Capone Became One of the World's Most Notorious Gangsters." History Hit. November 10, 2020. https://www.historyhit.com/gangster-profiles-al-capone.

USDA Forest Service "Huron-Manistee National Forest." https://www.fs.usda.gov/hmnf.

U.S. Fish and Wildlife Service. *Michigan's Recovery Implementation Strategy for Eastern Massasauga.* Updated March 4, 2020. https://www.fws.gov/sites/default/files/documents/FINAL%20MI%20EMR%20RIS_4Mar2020.pdf.

Walker, Emma. "14 Out of 36 Types of Goth Discussed with Their Common Traits and Features." *Inspire Uplift* (blog). Last updated October 18, 2022. https://blog.inspireuplift.com/types-of-goth.

Wantz, Terry, ed. "John A. Brooks." *Newaygo County Society of History & Genealogy Quarterly* (Winter & Spring. 1984).

WebMD Care. "Grant Medical Center." https://doctor.webmd.com.

What Is Goth? https://whatisgoth.com.

Wikipedia. "Black Dog (Folklore)." https://en.wikipedia.org.

———. "Briar Hill." https://en.wikipedia.org.

———. "Church Grim." https://en.wikipedia.org.

———. "Civilian Conservation Corps (CCC)." https://en.wikipedia.org.

———. "Croton Dam (Michigan)." https://en.wikipedia.org.

———. "Croton Township, Michigan." https://en.wikipedia.org.

———. "Culture-Bound Disorder." https://en.wikipedia.org.

———. "Fremont, Michigan." https://en.wikipedia.org.

———. "Grant Depot and Water Tower." https://en.wikipedia.org.

———. "Grant, Michigan." https://en.wikipedia.org.

———. "Manistee National Forest." https://en.wikipedia.org.

———. "Muskegon River." https://en.wikipedia.org.

———. "Newaygo, Michigan." https://en.wikipedia.org.

———. "Snakes in Mythology." https://en.wikipedia.org.

———. "White Cloud, Michigan." https://en.wikipedia.org.

Wilkinson, Tom. "Topology: Pub." Architectural Review, September 15, 2016. https://www.architectural-review.com.

Yelp. "Brew Works." https://www.yelp.com/biz/brew-works-fremont.

About the Author

Before moving to Michigan when she was quite young, Marie Cisneros was raised in South Texas, where she and her family lived on the outskirts of Laredo, in a barrio known as Ghost Town. Family outings included exploring the foothills and brushlands nearby, where they would often find Clovis points or other interesting objects, once discovering the bleached bones of a human hand. This was the beginning of her need to search, to explore and find out about all things mysterious, hidden or unknown. At the prophetic age of thirteen, she picked up her first books on ghosts, astrology, magic and UFOlogy. Thus her quest into the mysterious world of the unknown and the paranormal began. Marie is an investigative journalist, professional astrologer, UFOlogist and Universal Life Church minister with an AAS and a BS in the medical sciences. Her personal interests include acrylic painting and mixed media art, and her art has been exhibited in local galleries. She is a former MUFON field investigator as well as a columnist for the *MUFON Journal*. She has been a guest and guest host on numerous UFOlogy and paranormal podcasts and radio and cable television broadcasts. She is currently an investigative journalist and astrologer for MuskegonChannel.com, an online media channel, hosting *Paranormal Muskegon* and *Muskegon by the Stars*.

Marie's search for answers in a world that seems to come out only in the dark of night has led her down many paths, some of them quite inexplicable and puzzling. Even so, it is that tantalizing search for anything hidden, enigmatic or paranormal that this girl from Ghost Town lives for.

FREE eBOOK OFFER

Scan the QR code below, enter your e-mail address and get our original Haunted America compilation eBook delivered straight to your inbox for free.

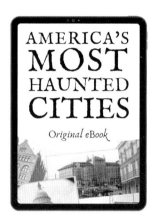

ABOUT THE BOOK

Every city, town, parish, community and school has their own paranormal history. Whether they are spirits caught in the Bardo, ancestors checking on their descendants, restless souls sending a message or simply spectral troublemakers, ghosts have been part of the human tradition from the beginning of time.

In this book, we feature a collection of stories from five of America's most haunted cities: Baltimore, Chicago, Galveston, New Orleans and Washington, D.C.

SCAN TO GET
AMERICA'S MOST HAUNTED CITIES

Having trouble scanning? Go to:
biz.arcadiapublishing.com/americas-most-haunted-cities

Visit us at
www.historypress.com
....